perhaps peruse while listening
in either sense of the word

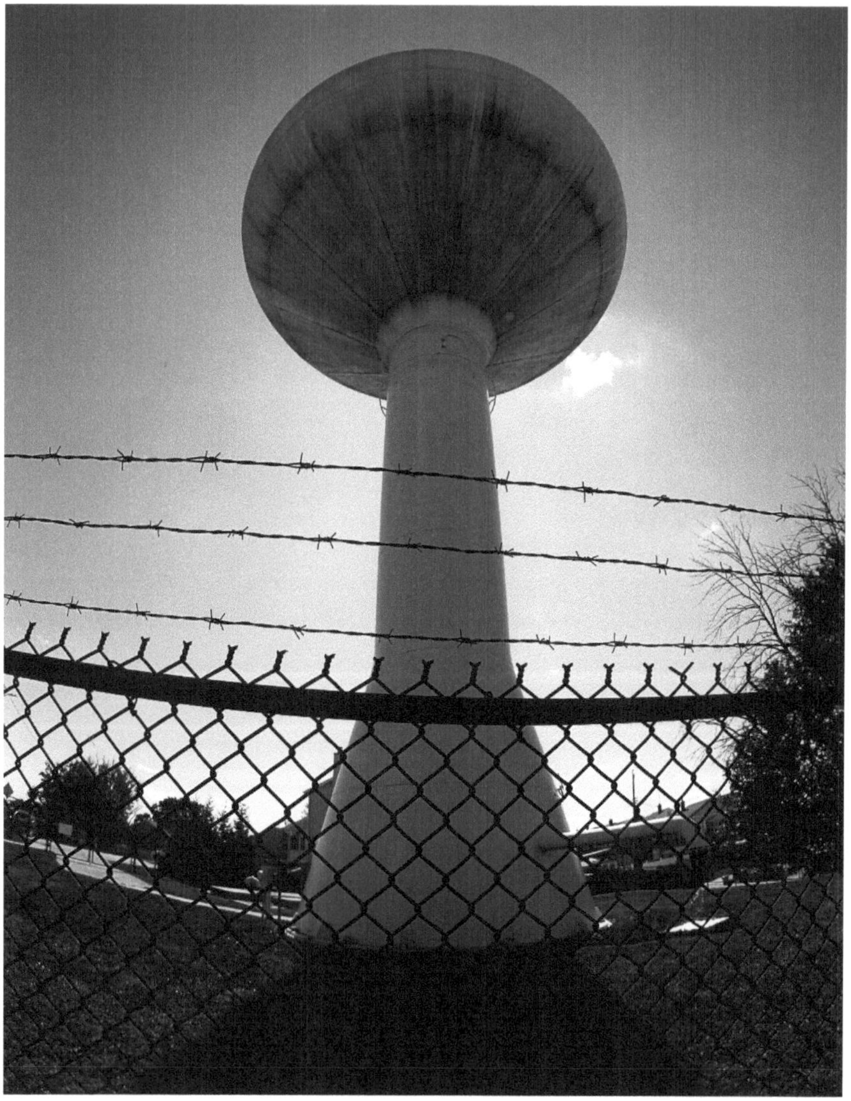

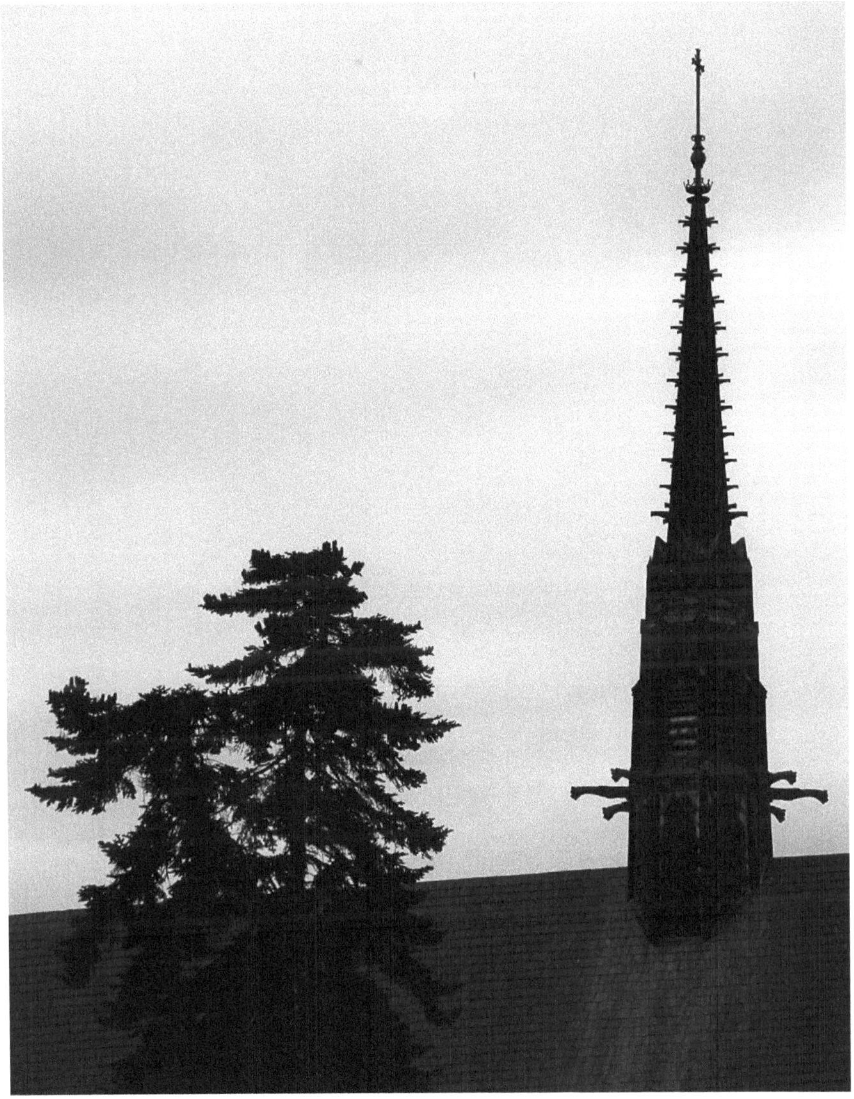

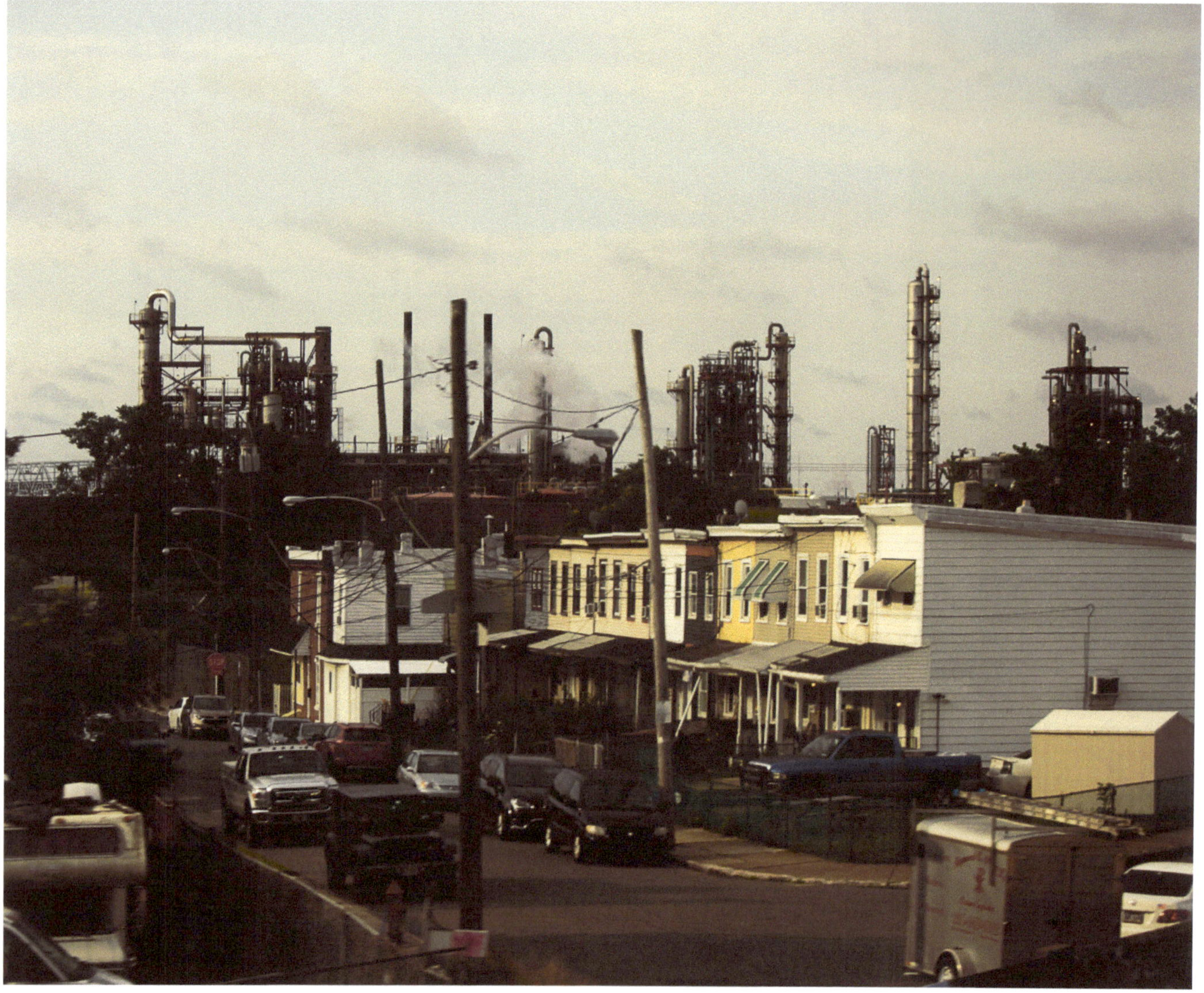

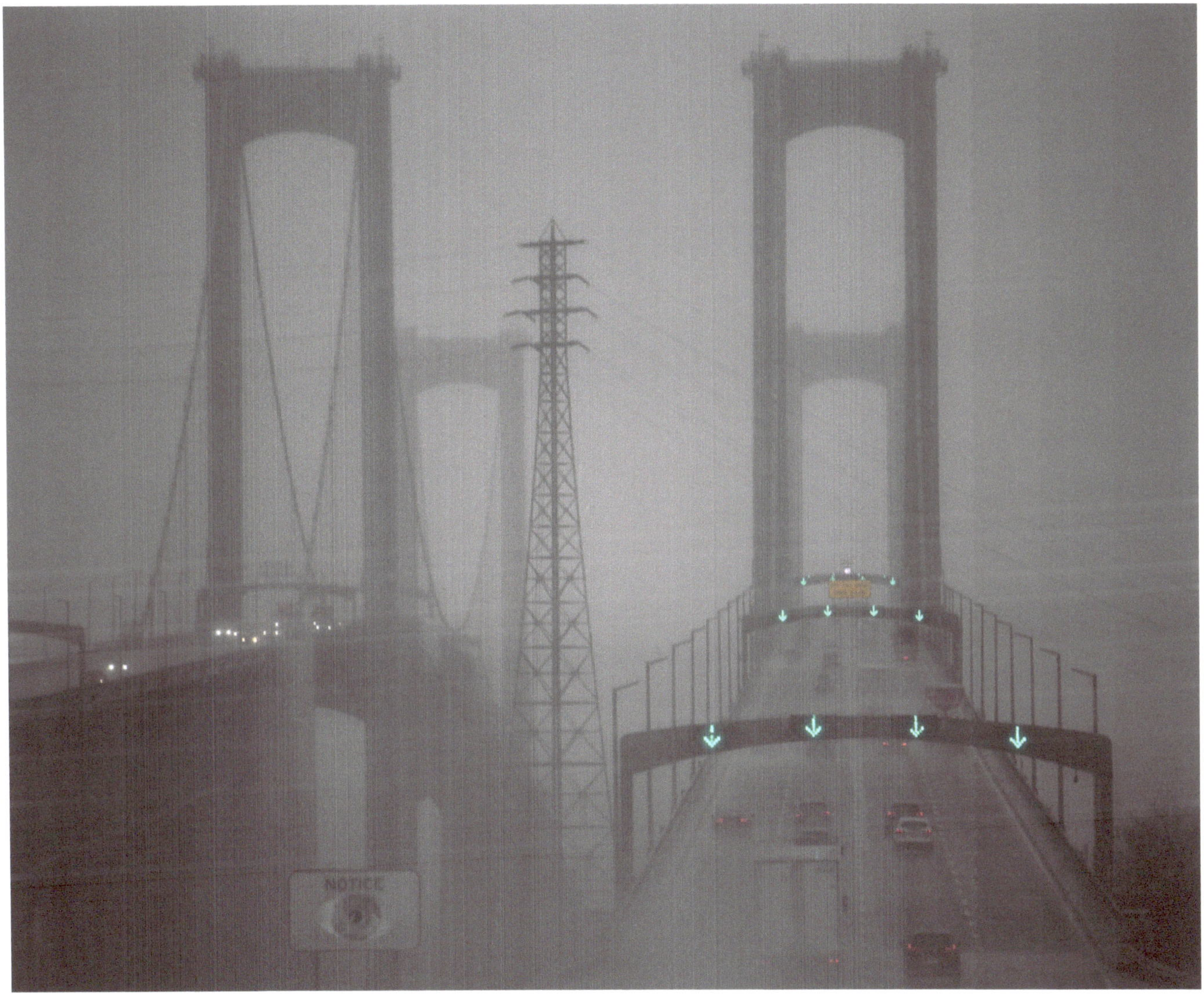
NOTICE

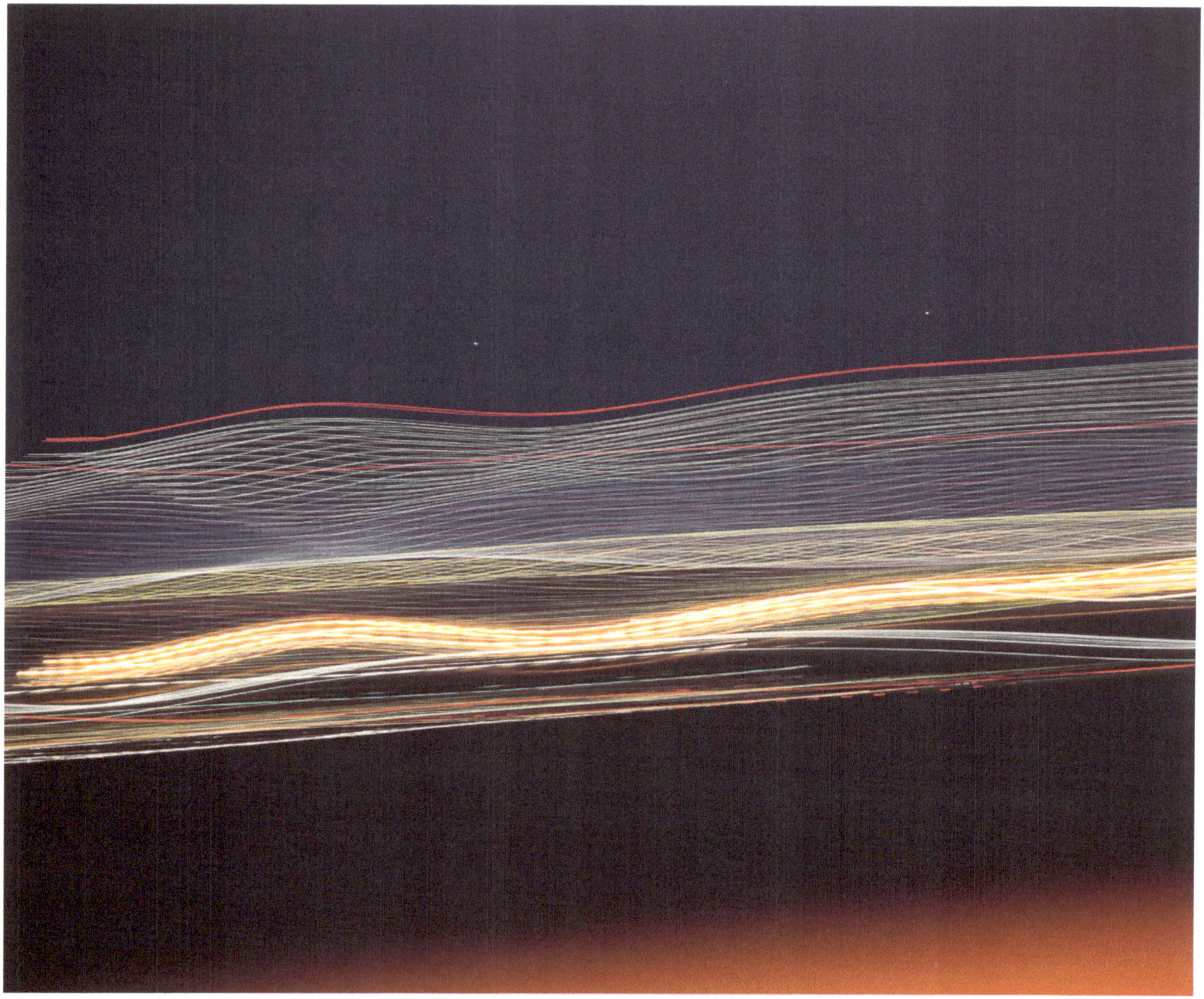

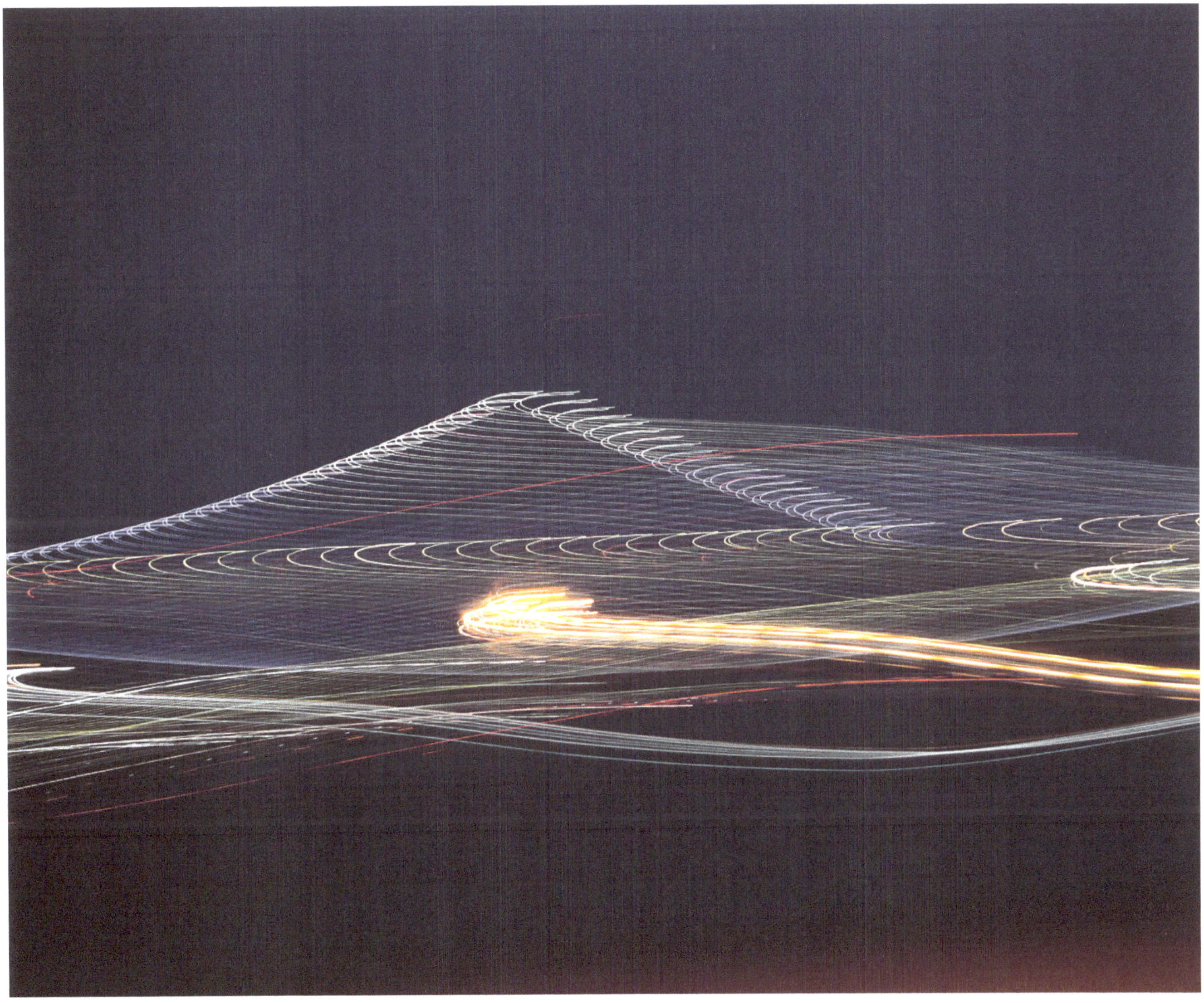

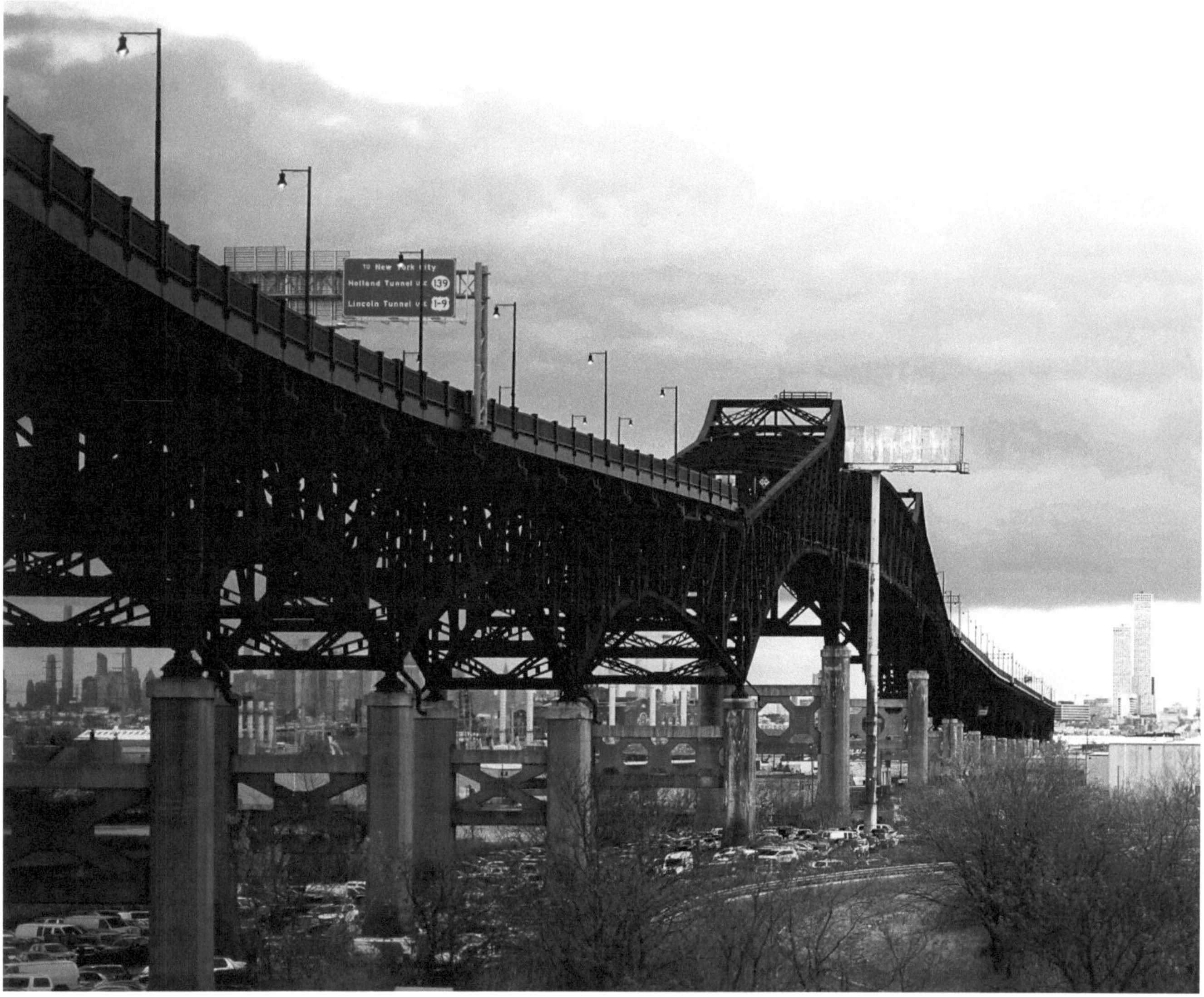
Holland Tunnel
139
Lincoln Tunnel
1-9

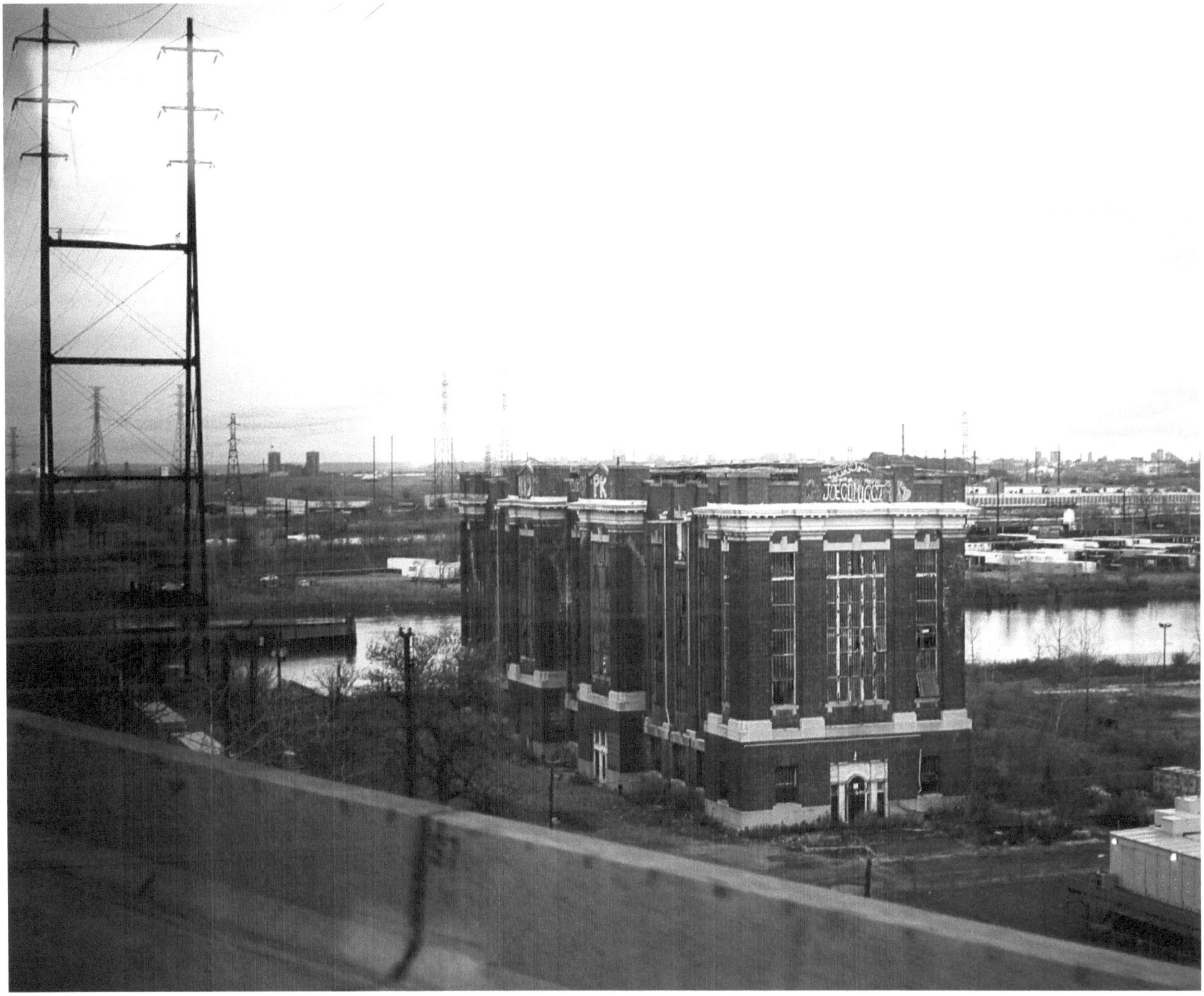

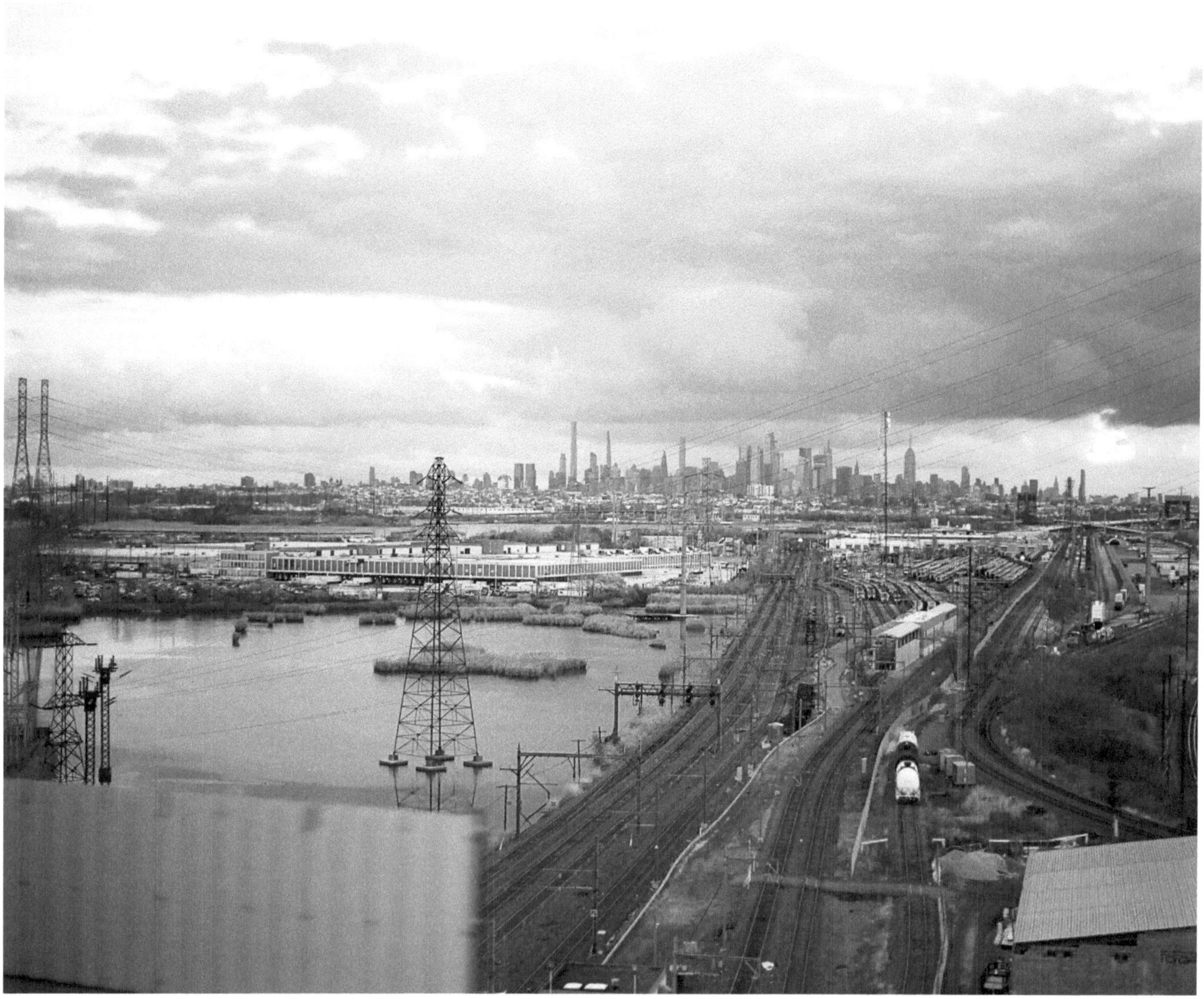

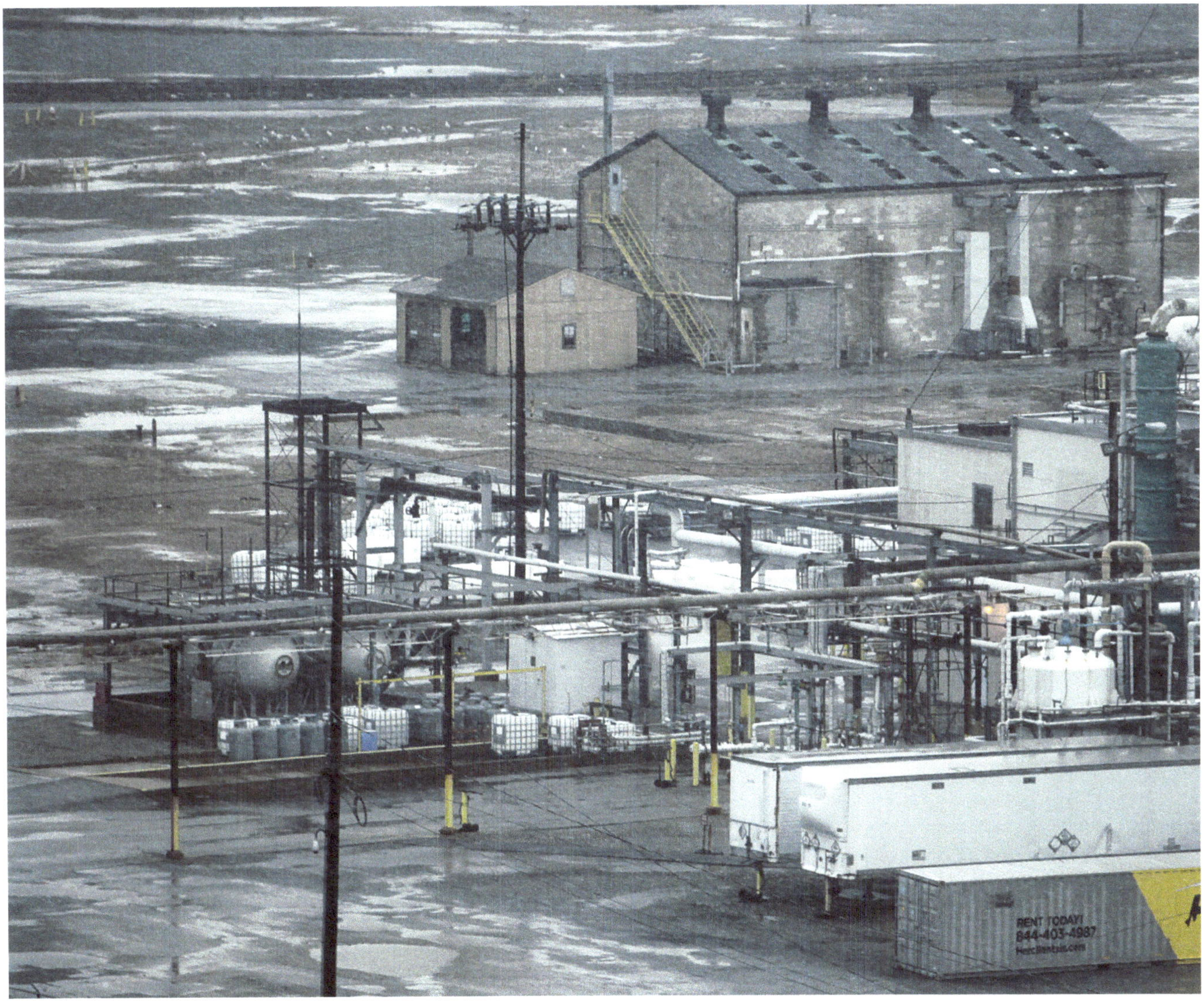
RENT TODAY!
844-403-4987

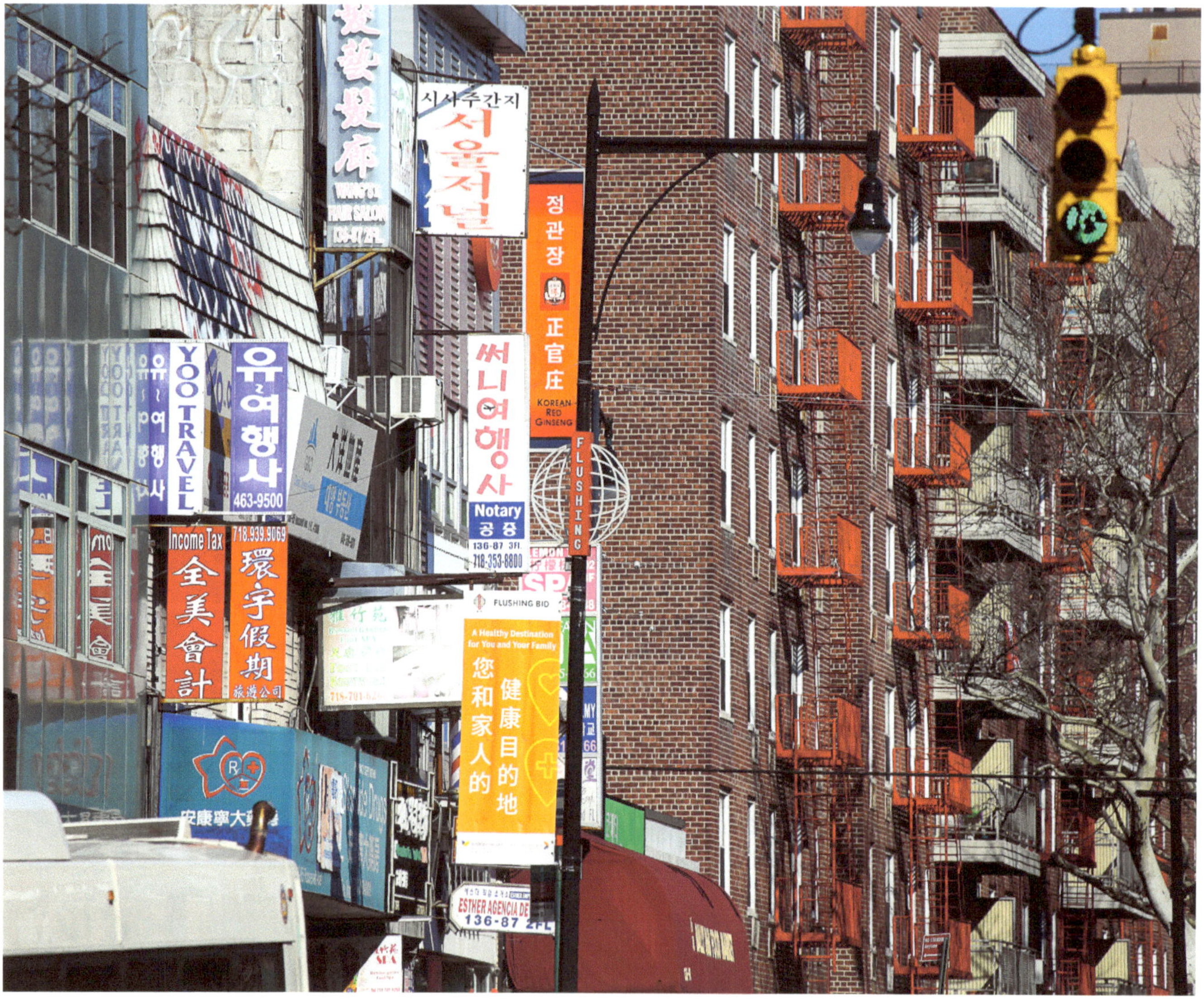
시사주간지
정관장
正官庄
KOREAN RED GINSENG
YOO TRAVEL
유여행사
463-9500
써니여행사
Notary
공증
136-87 3Fl.
718-353-8800
FLUSHING
Income Tax
全美會計
718.939.9069
環宇假期
旅遊公司
FLUSHING BID
A Healthy Destination for You and Your Family
您和家人的
健康目的地
ESTHER AGENCIA DE
136-87 2FL

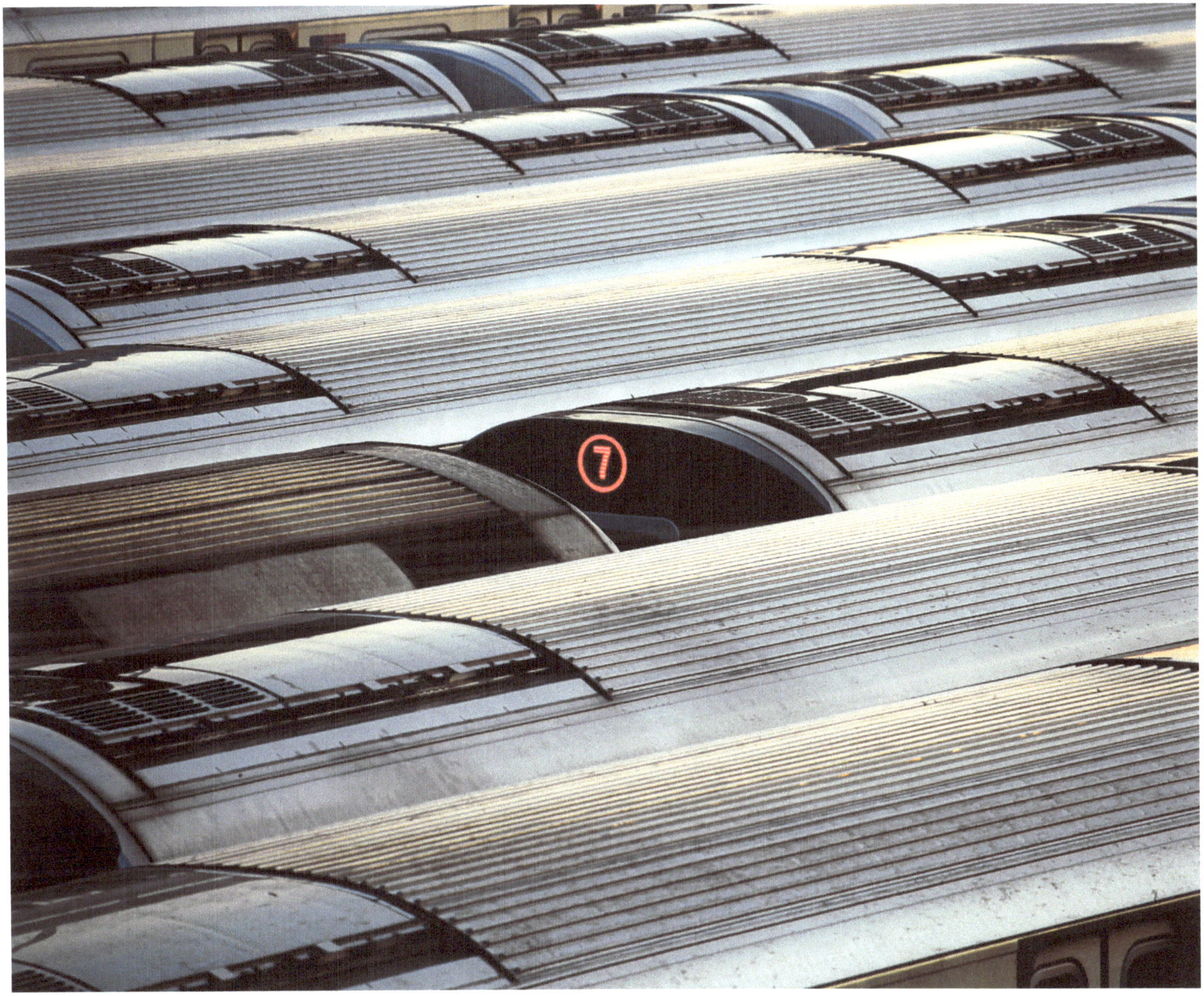
7

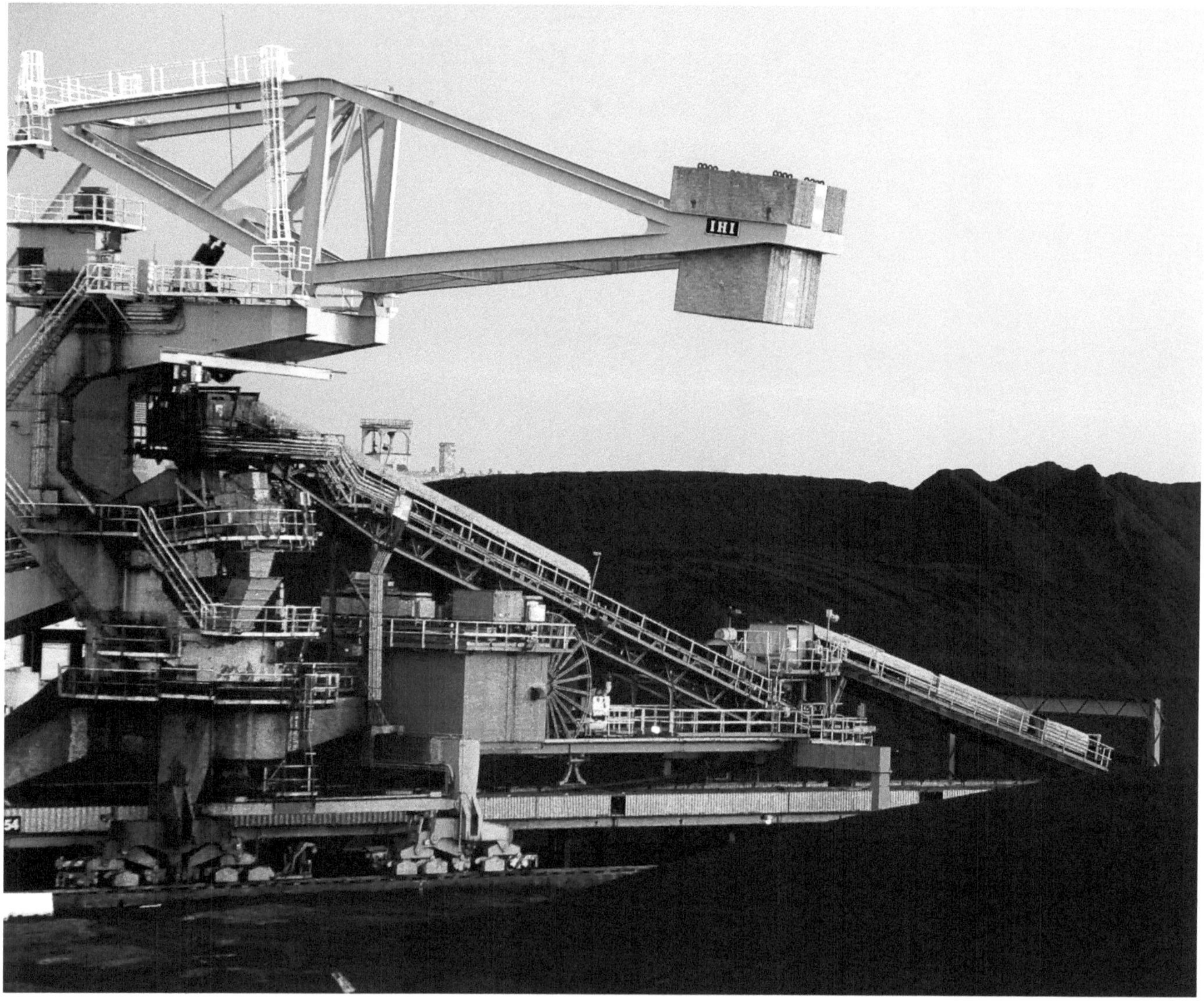
IHI

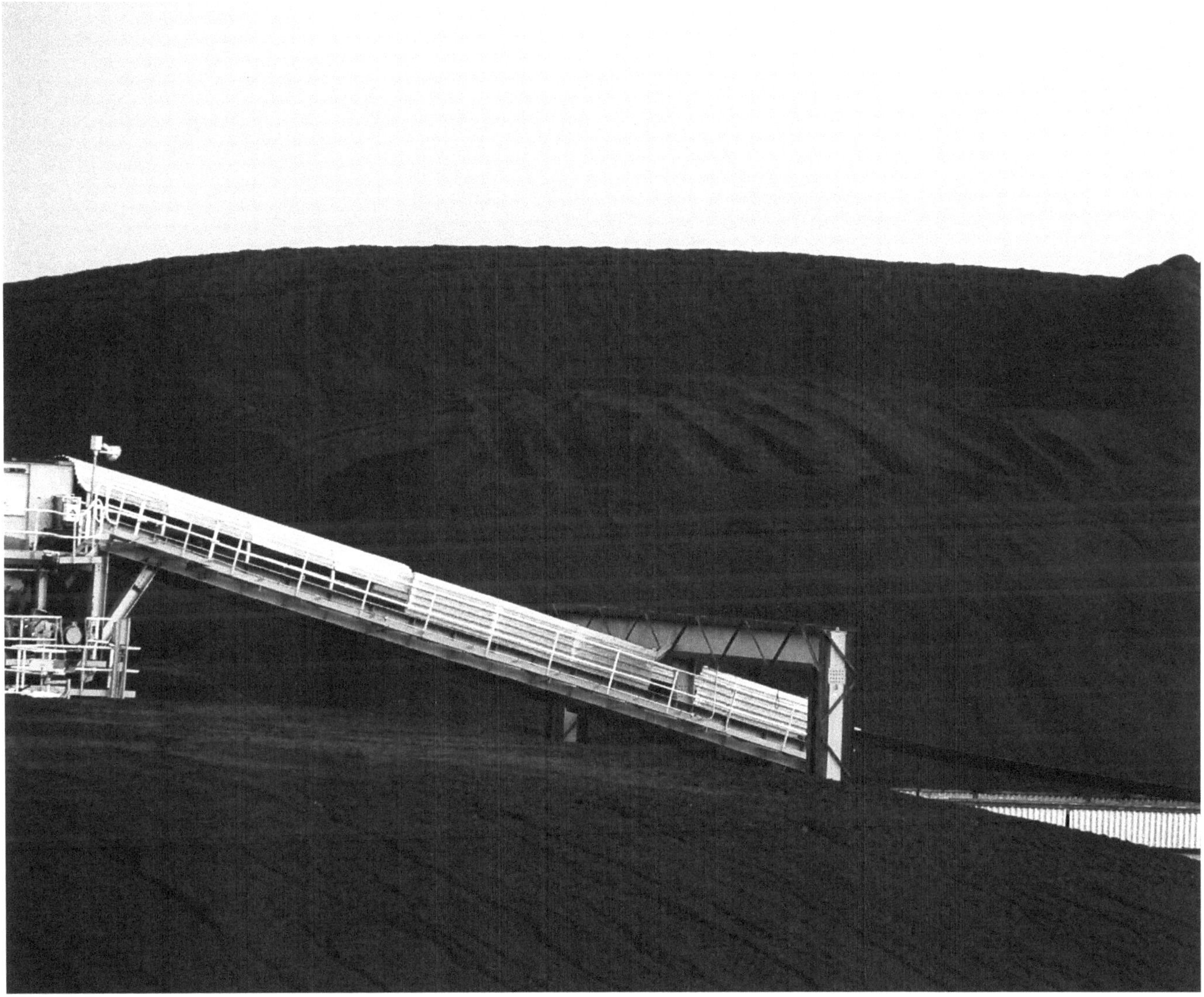

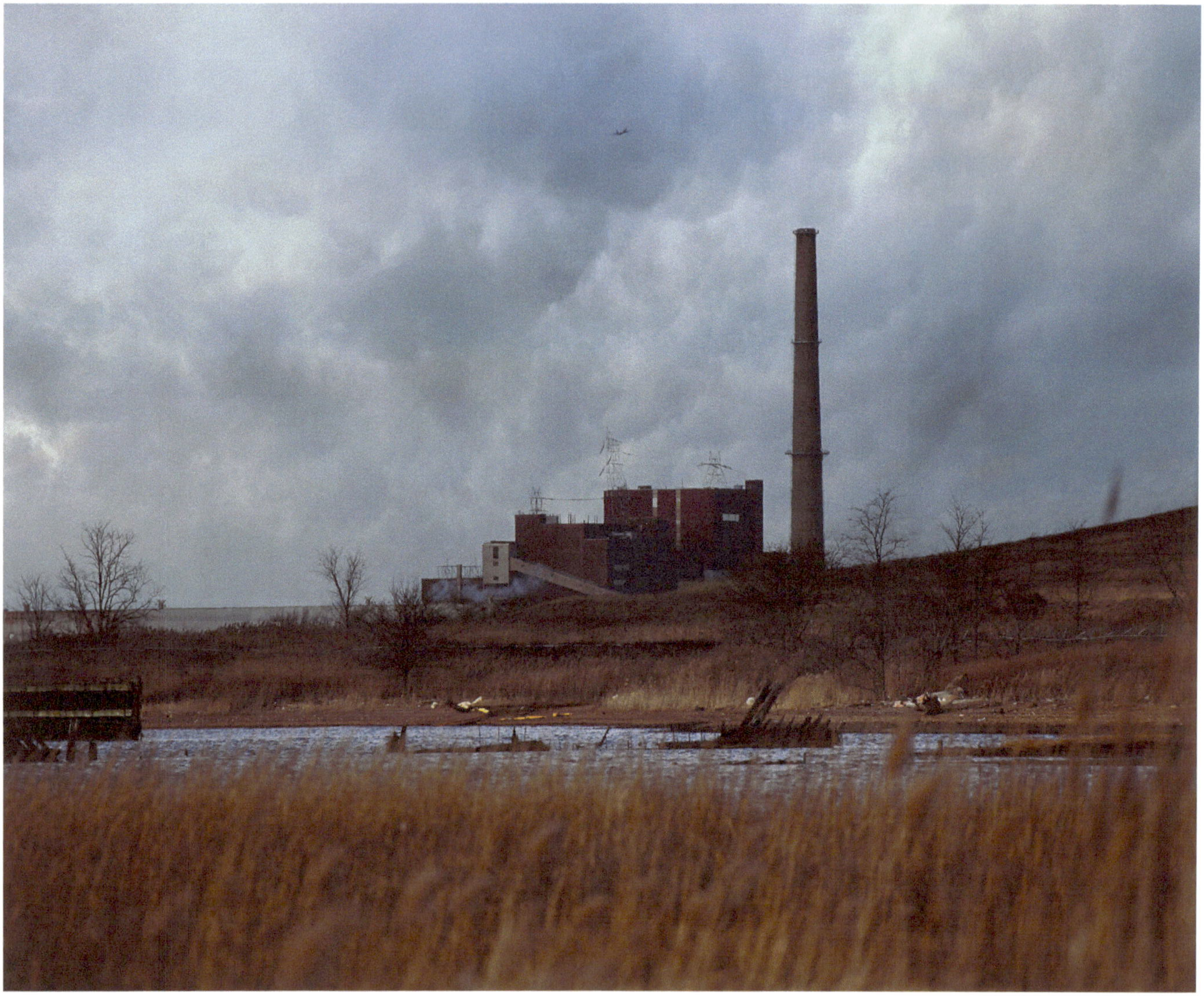

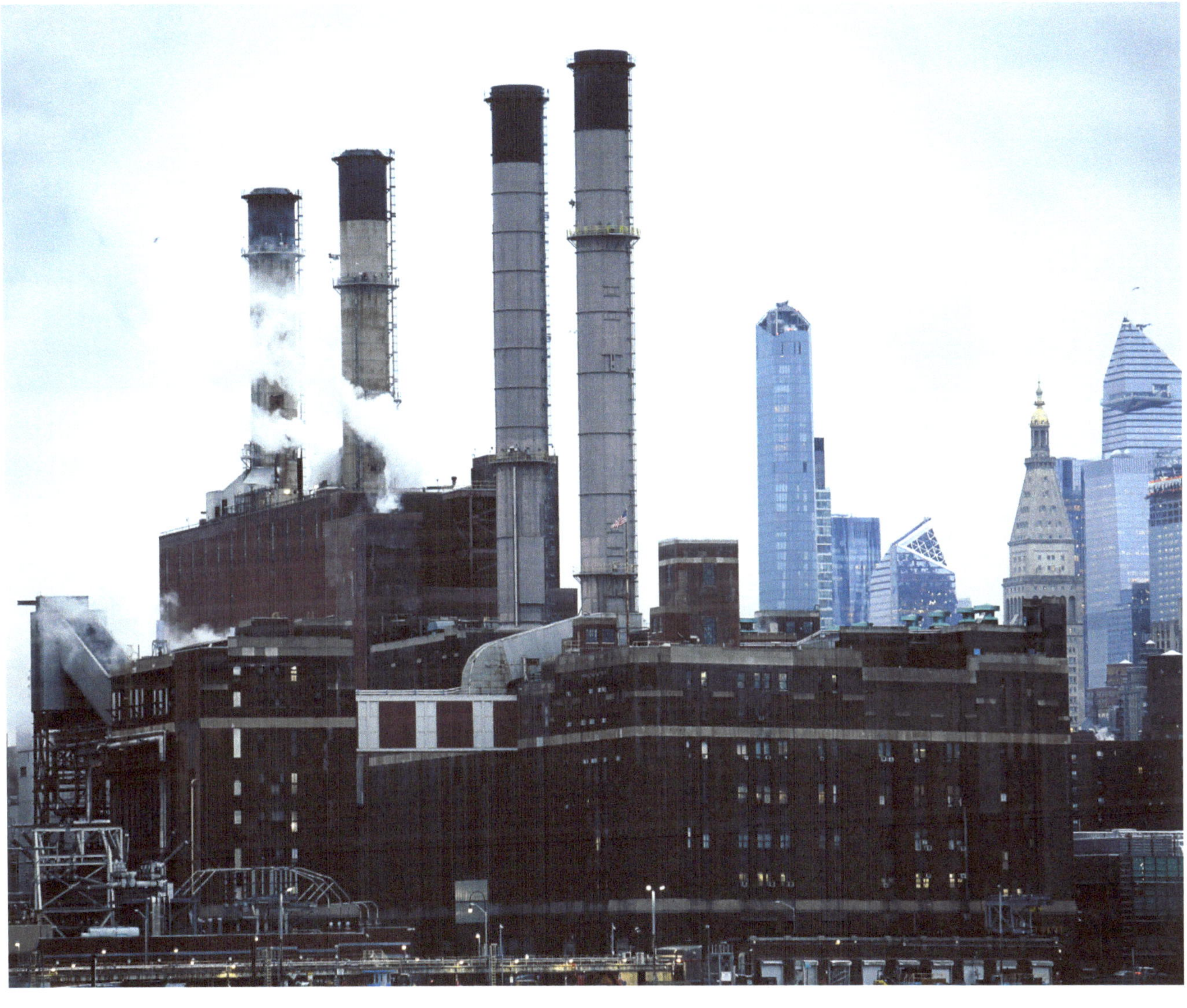

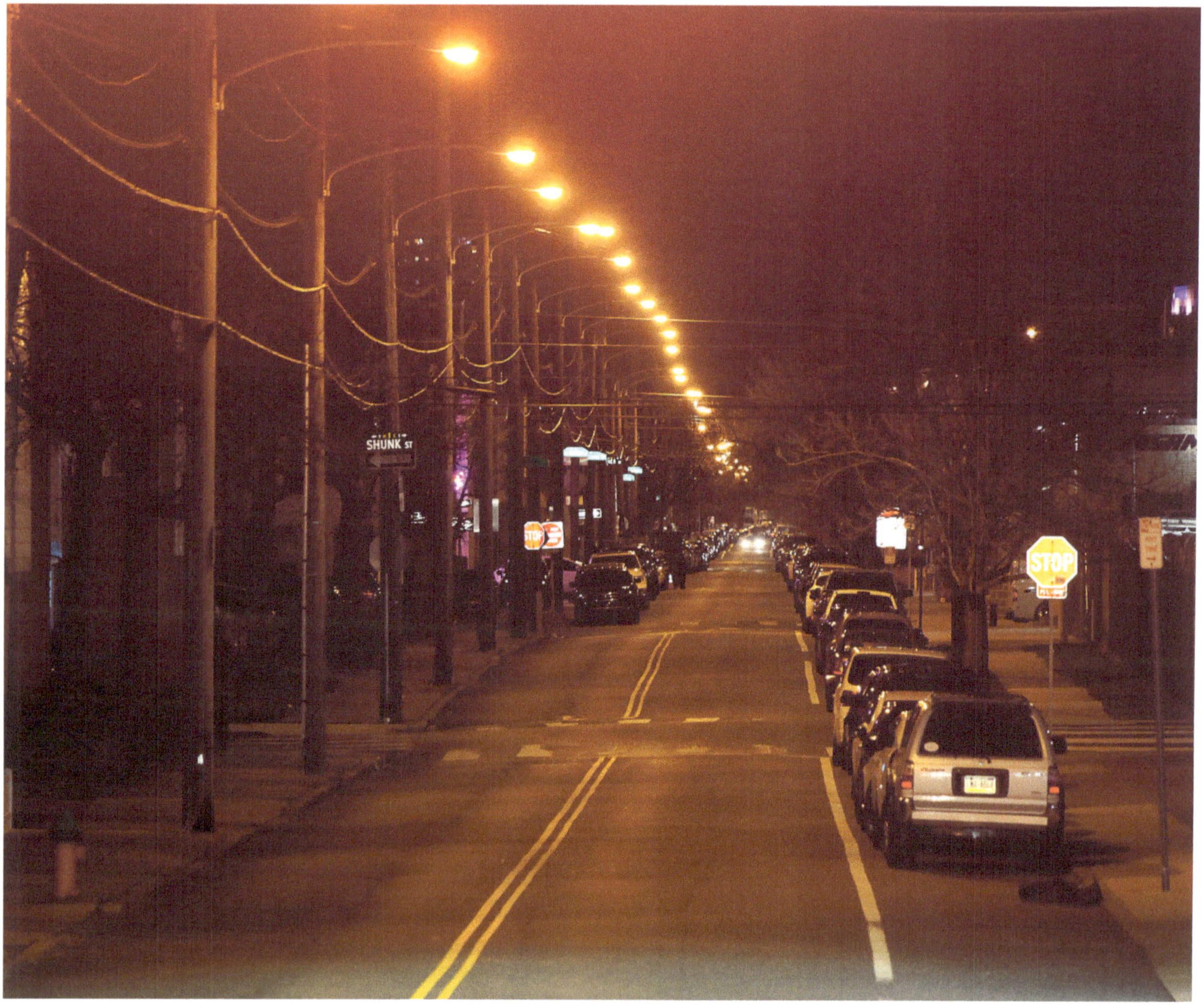
SHUNK ST
STOP

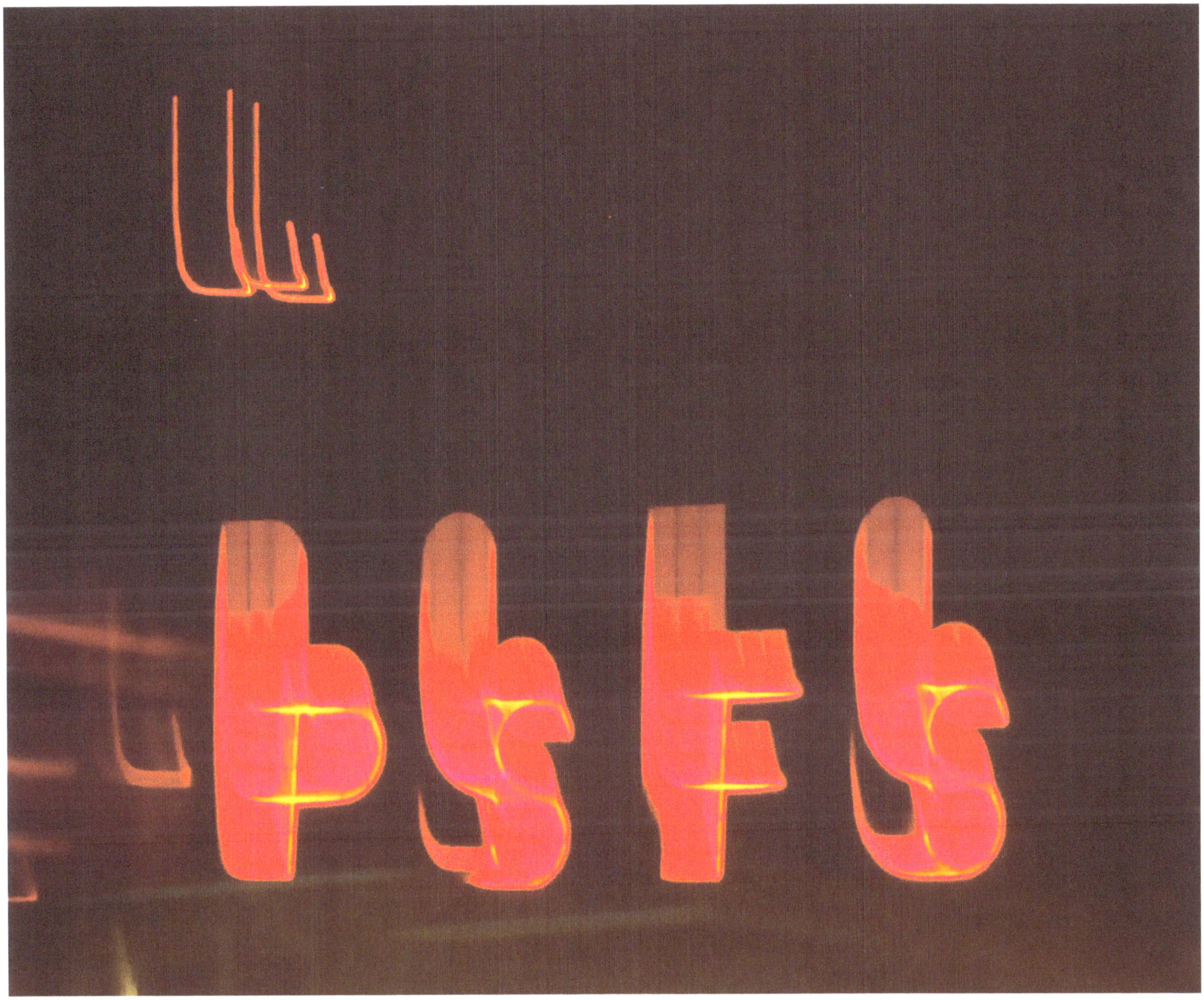
PSFS

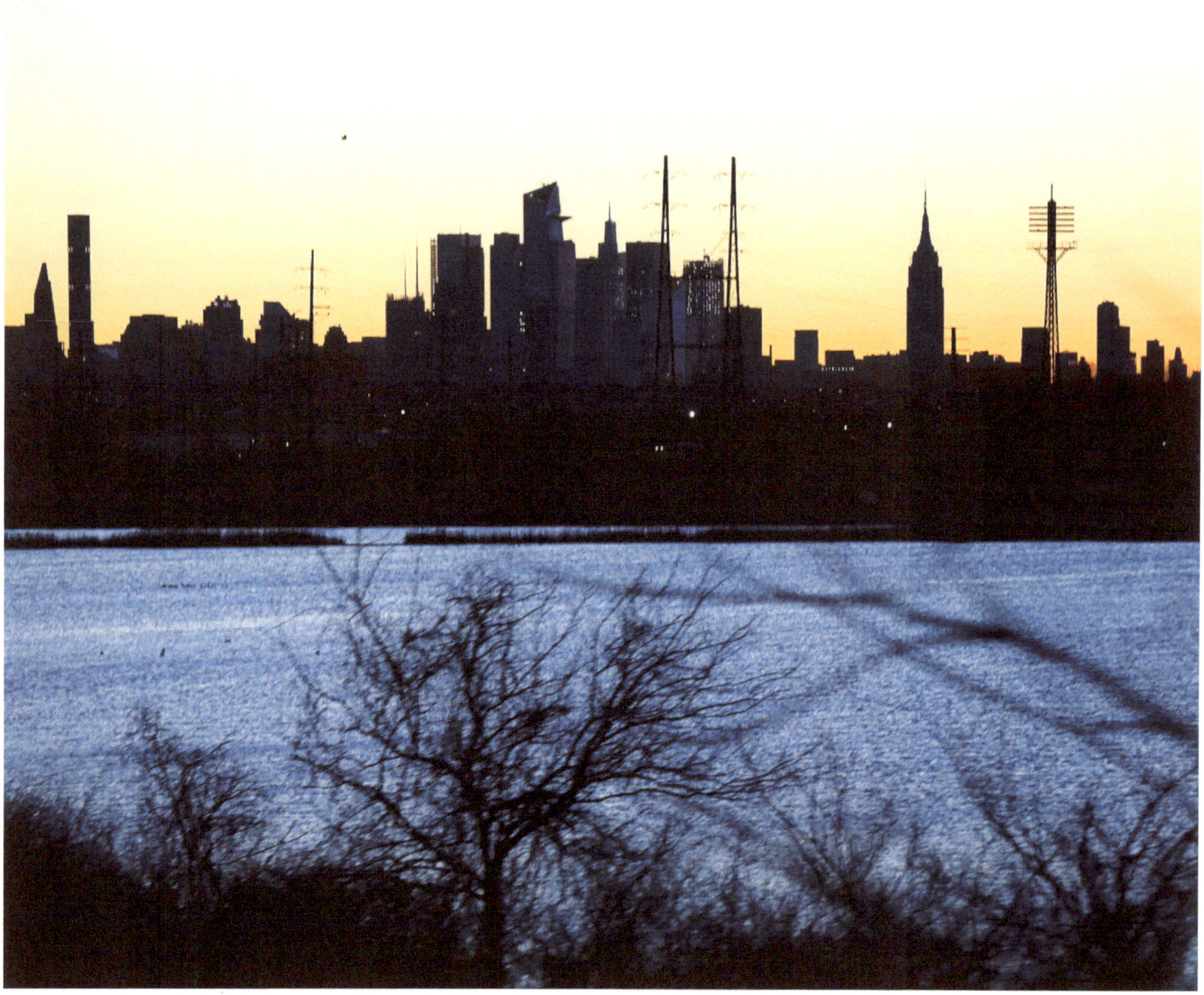

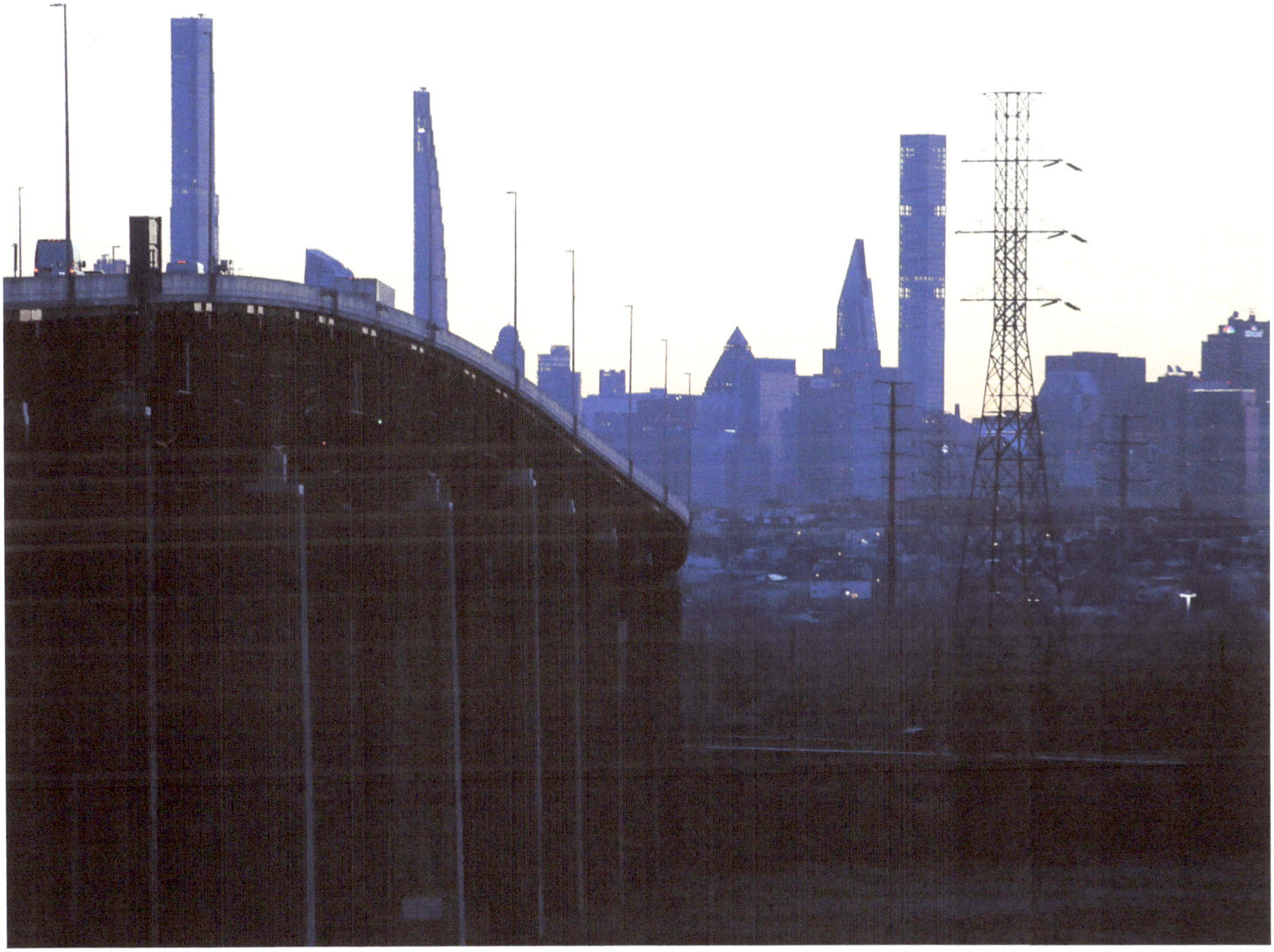

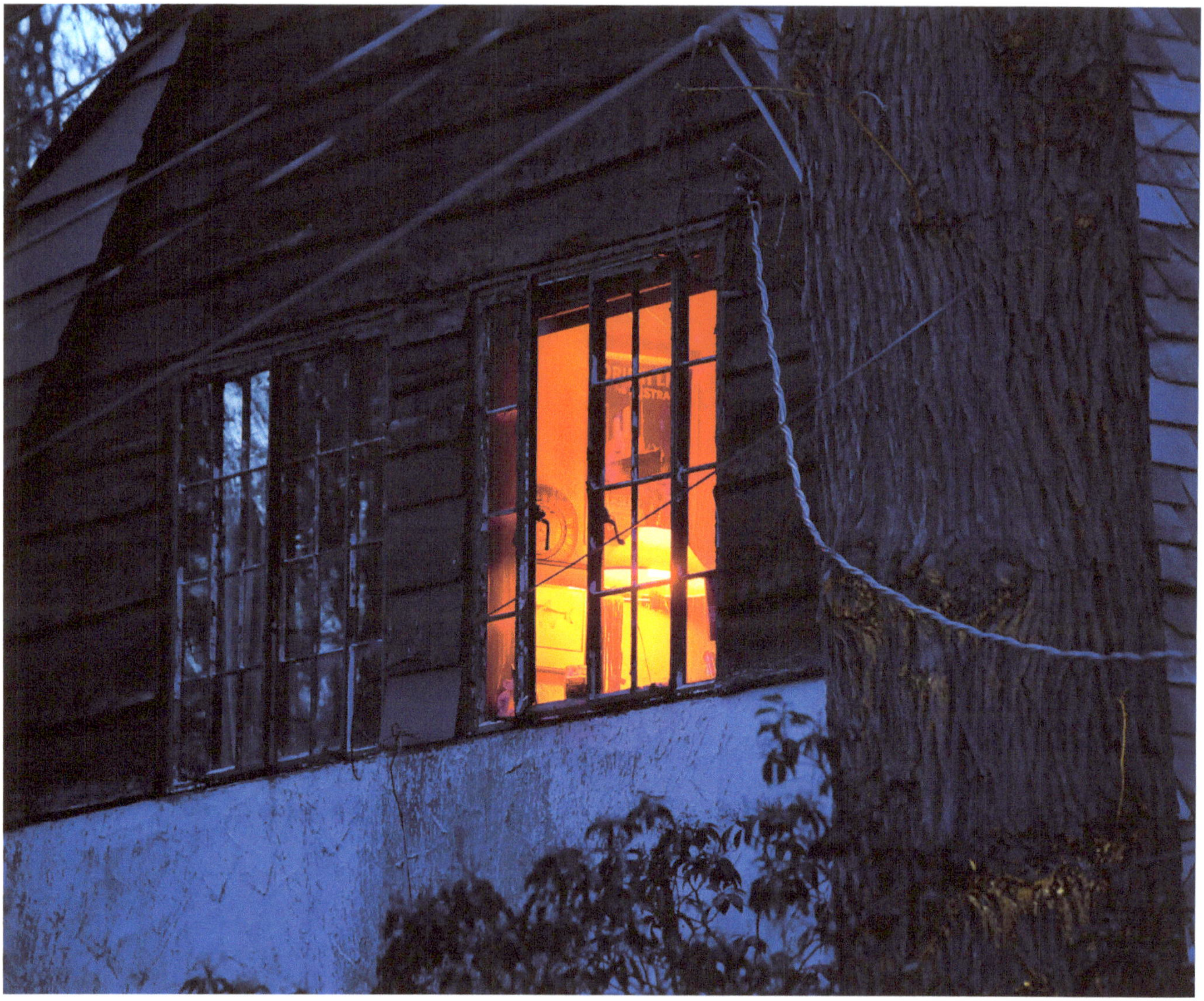

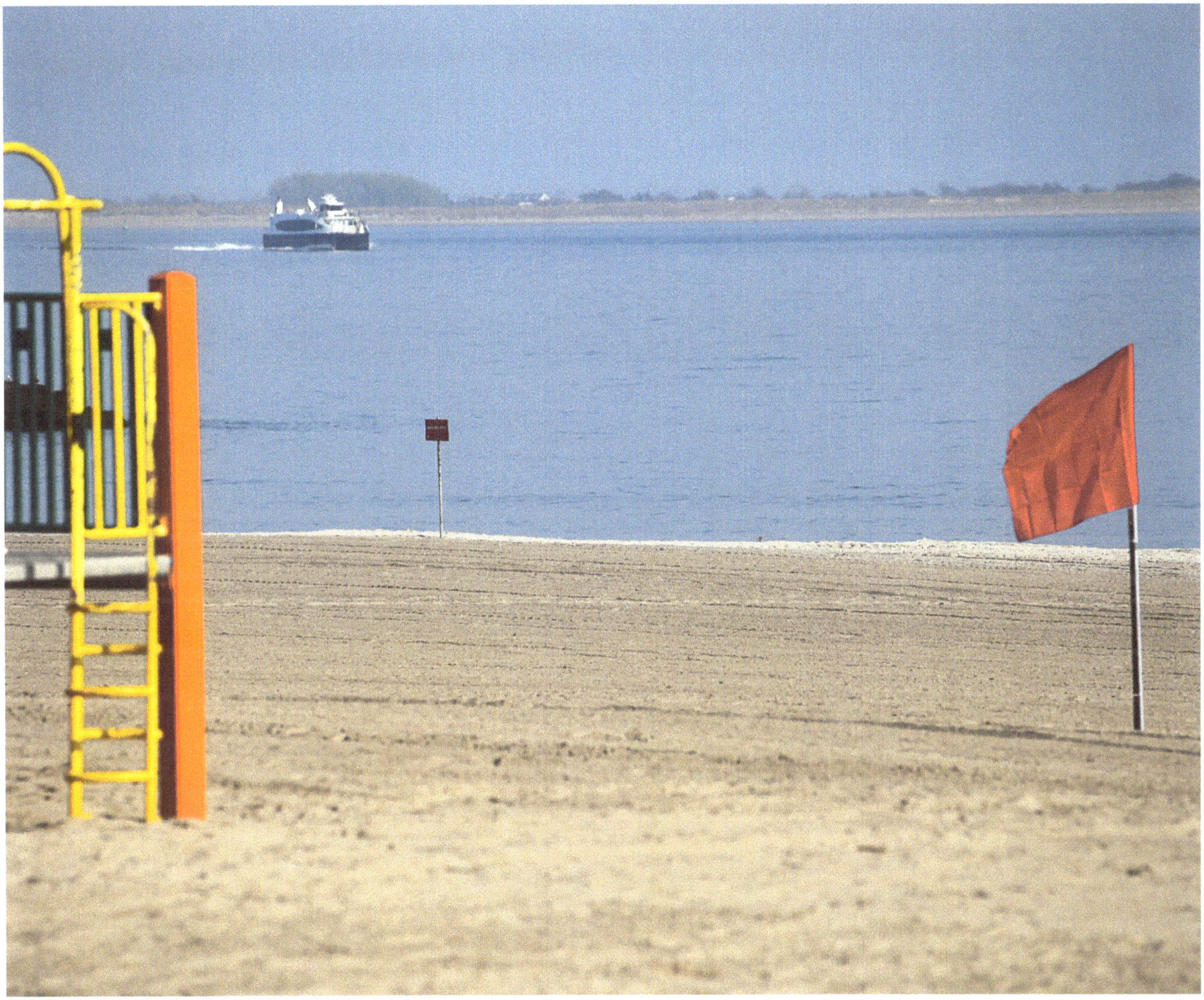

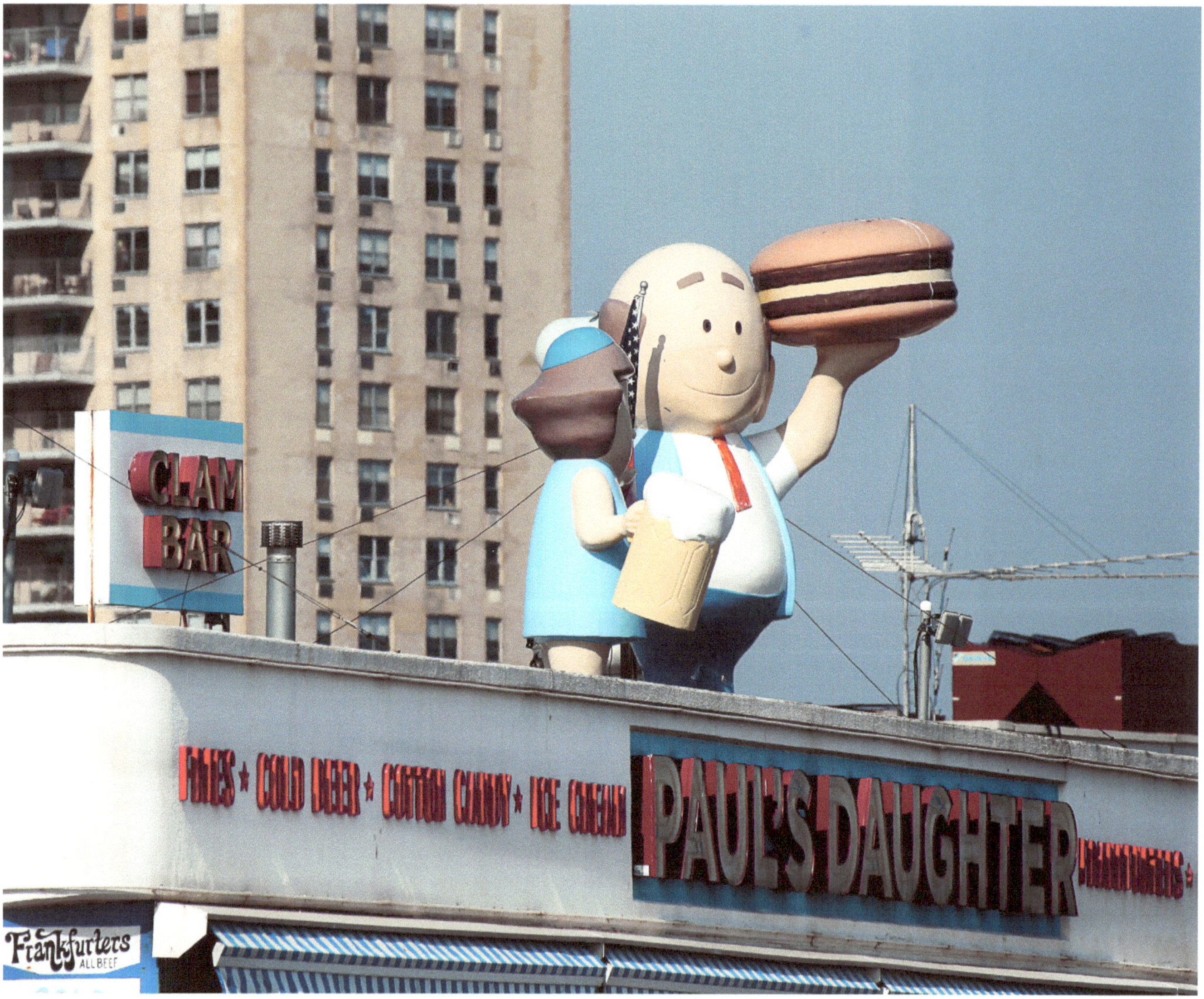
CLAM
BAR
FRIES ★ COLD BEER ★ COTTON CANDY ★ ICE CREAM
PAUL'S DAUGHTER
Frankfurters
ALL BEEF

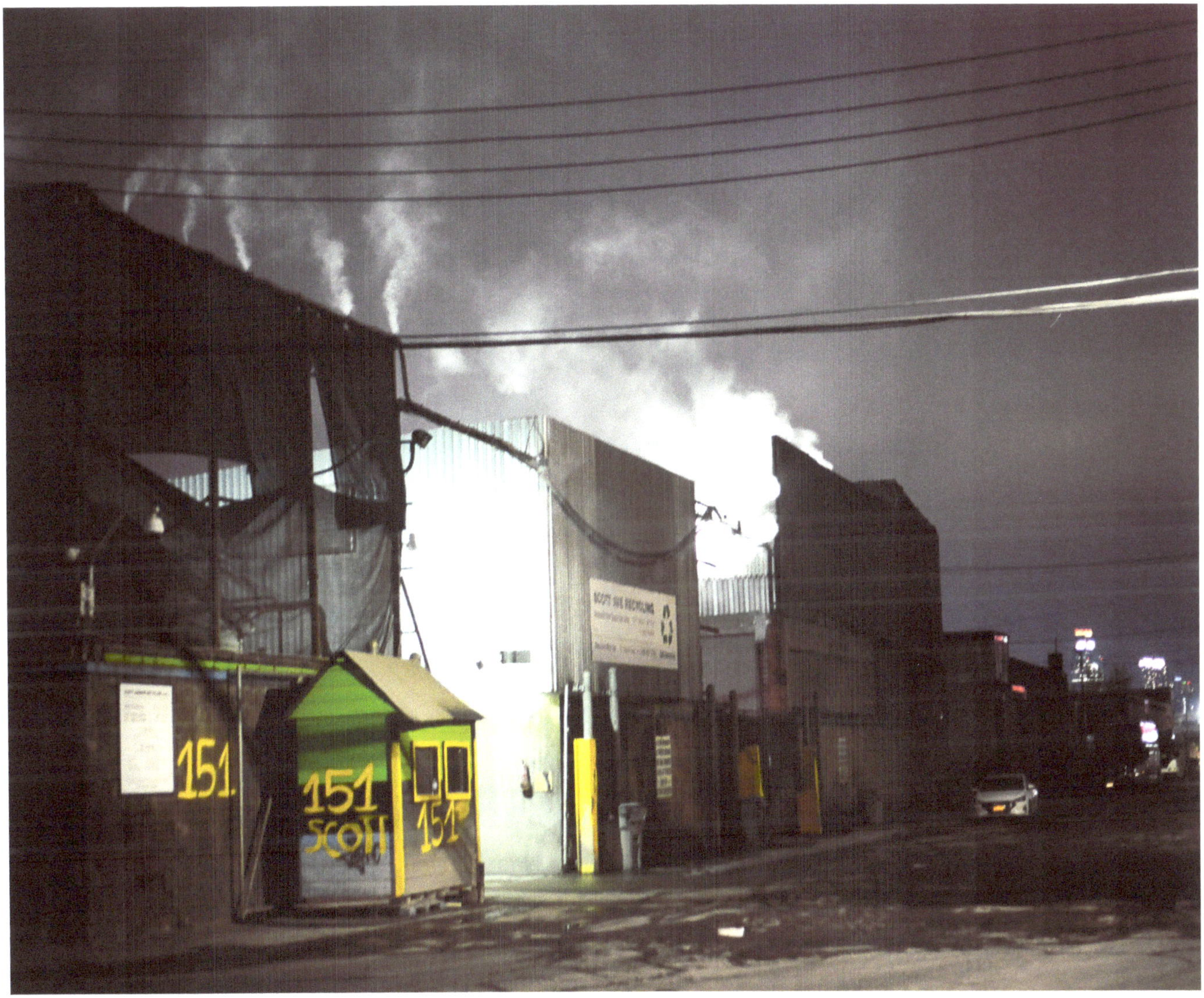
151
151
SCOTT
151

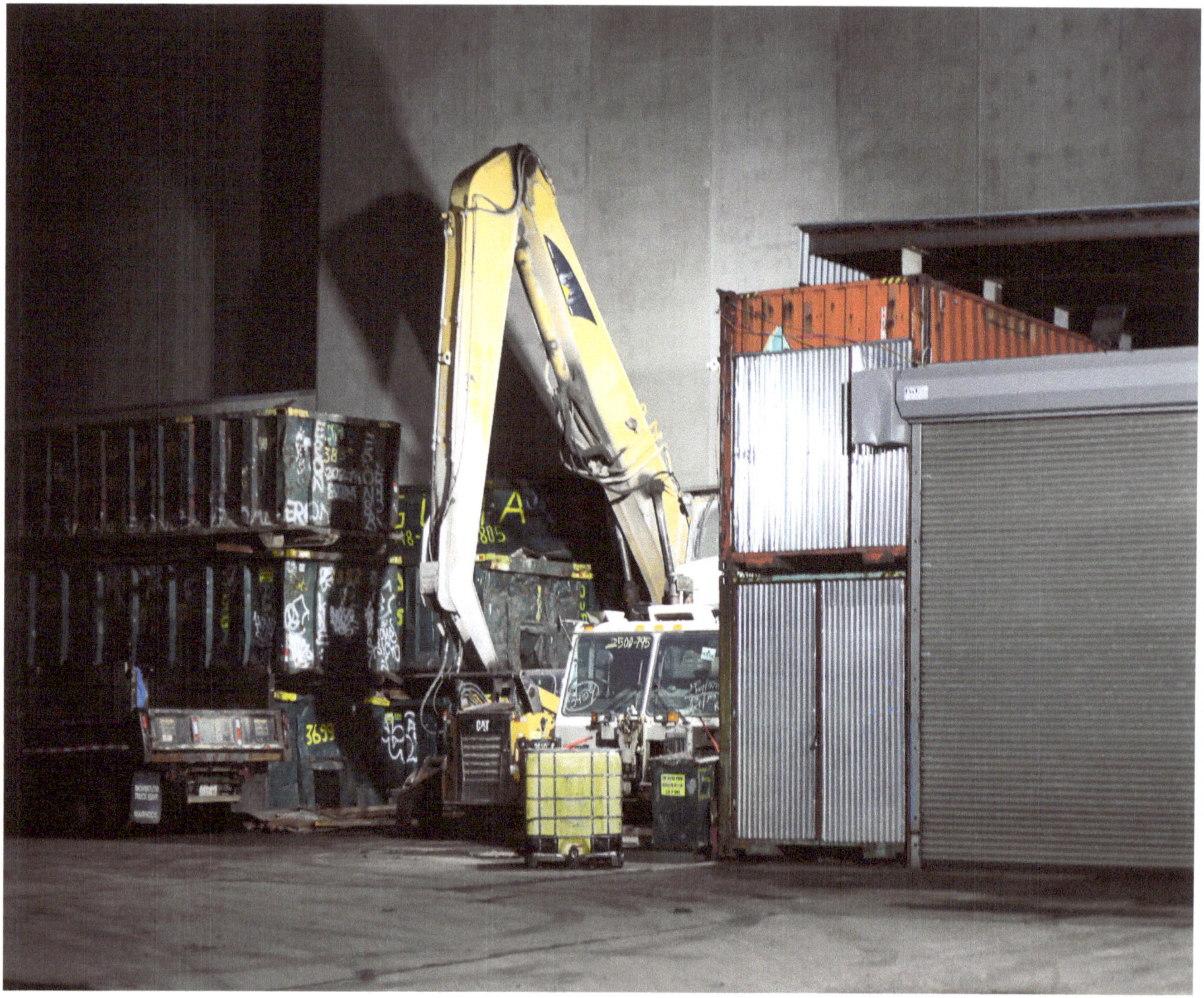
CAT

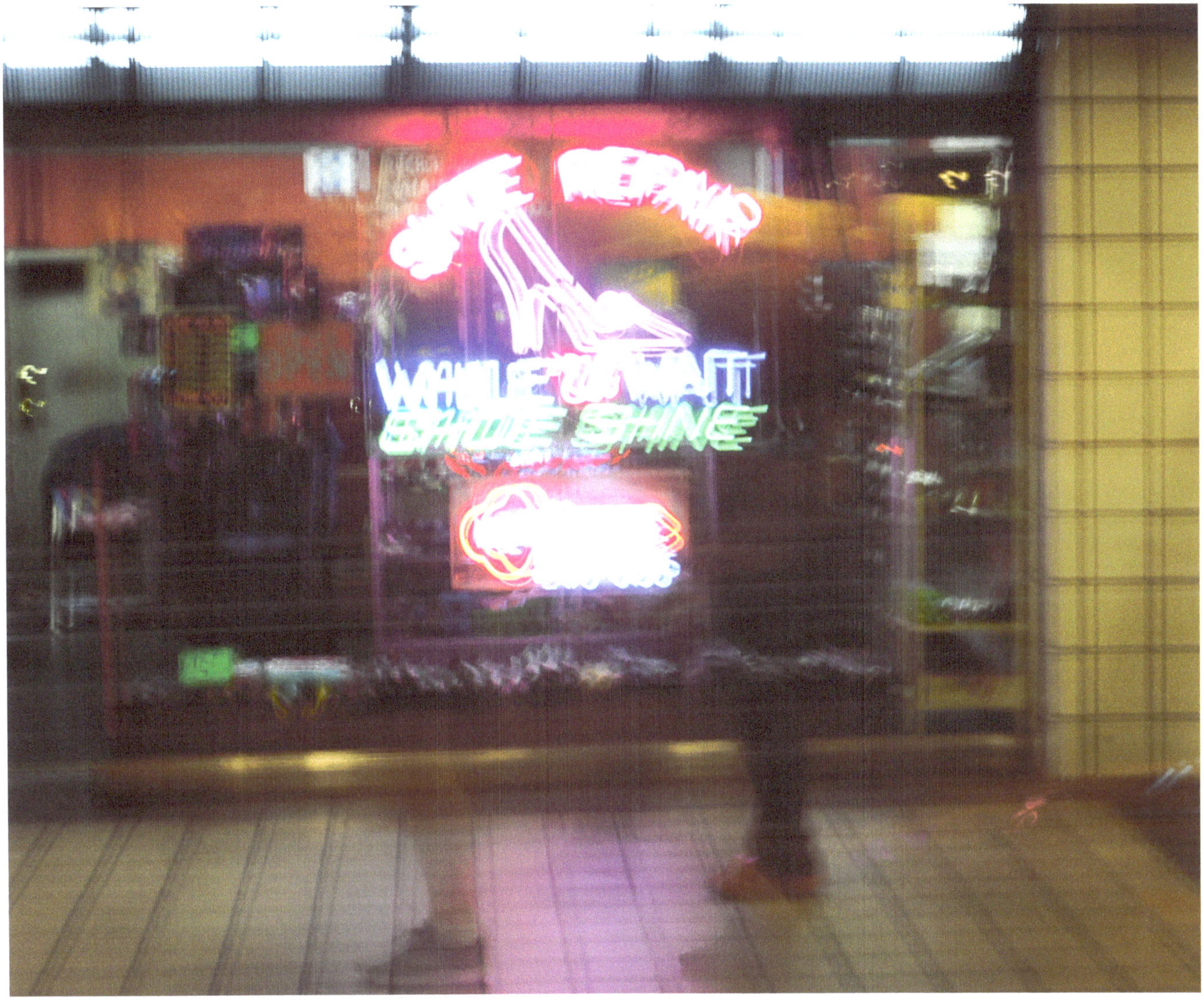
WHILE U WAIT
SHOE SHINE

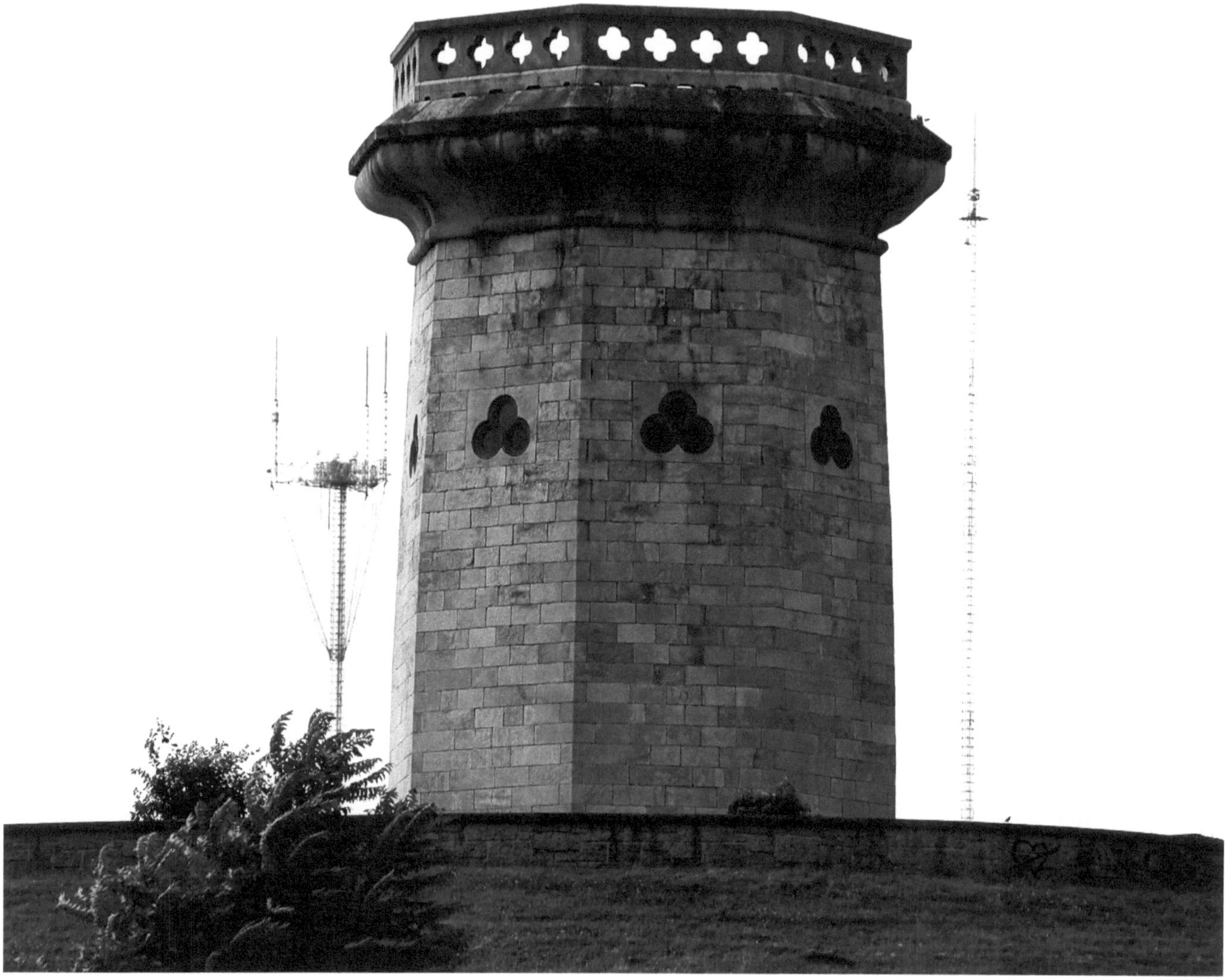

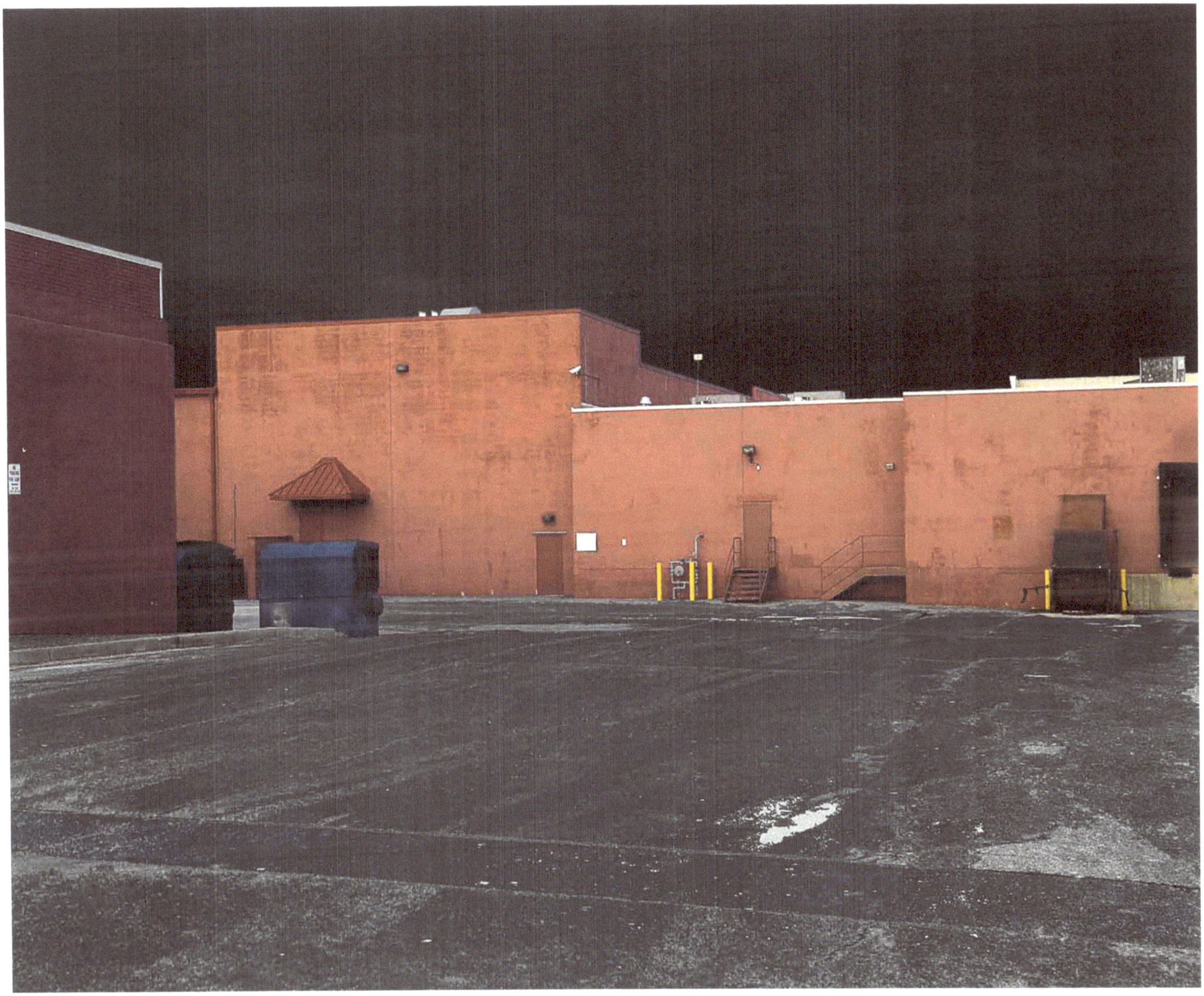

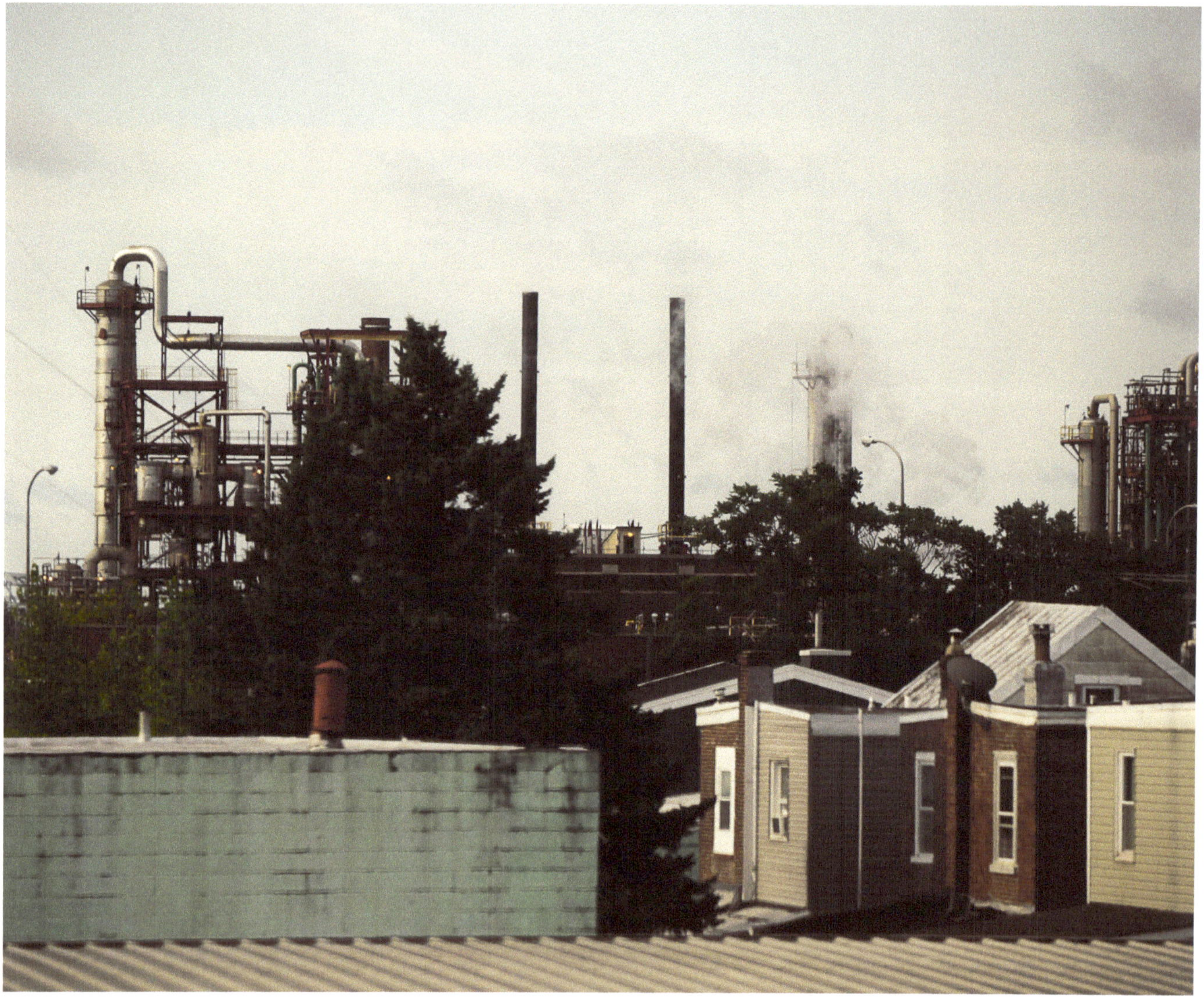

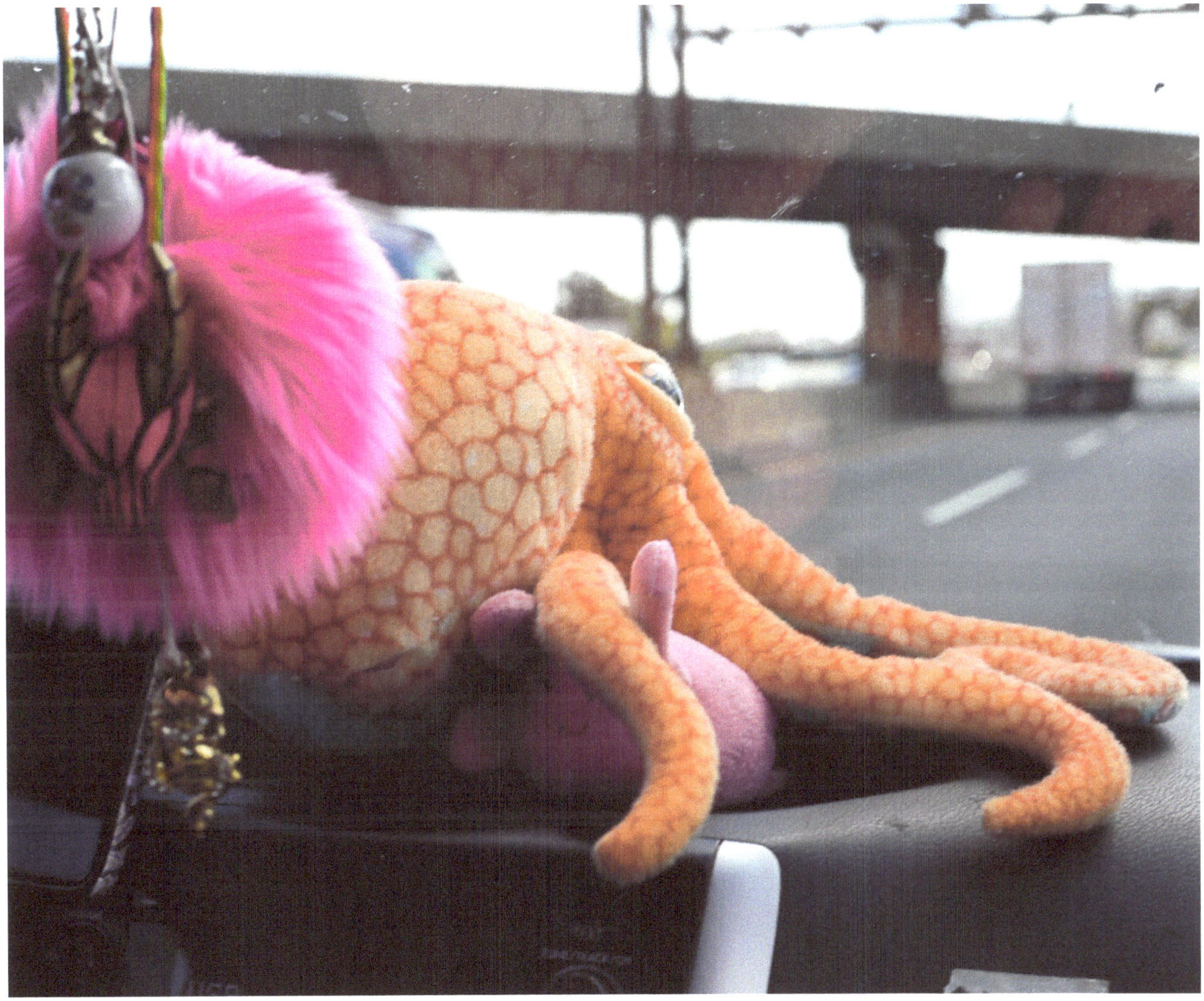

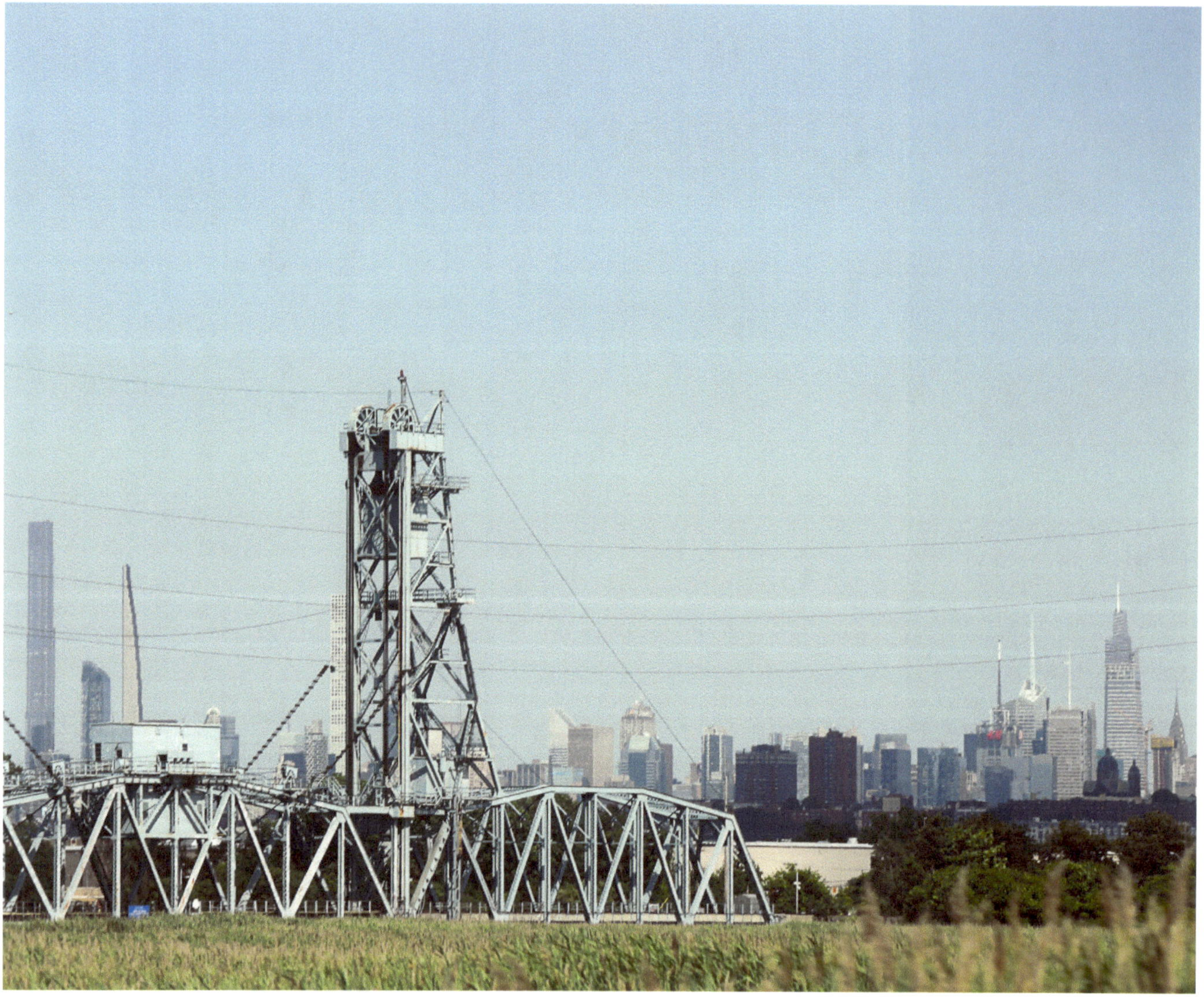

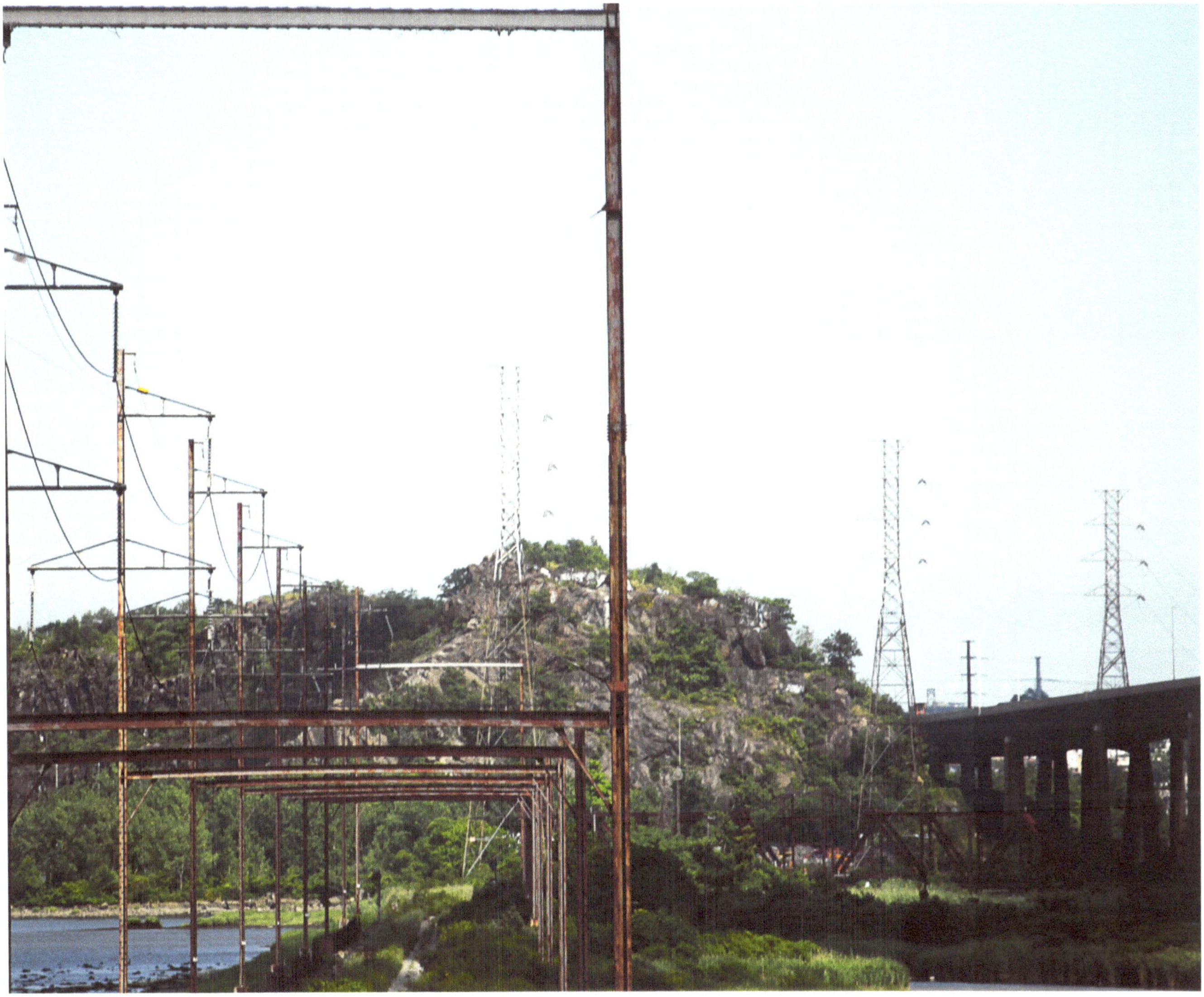

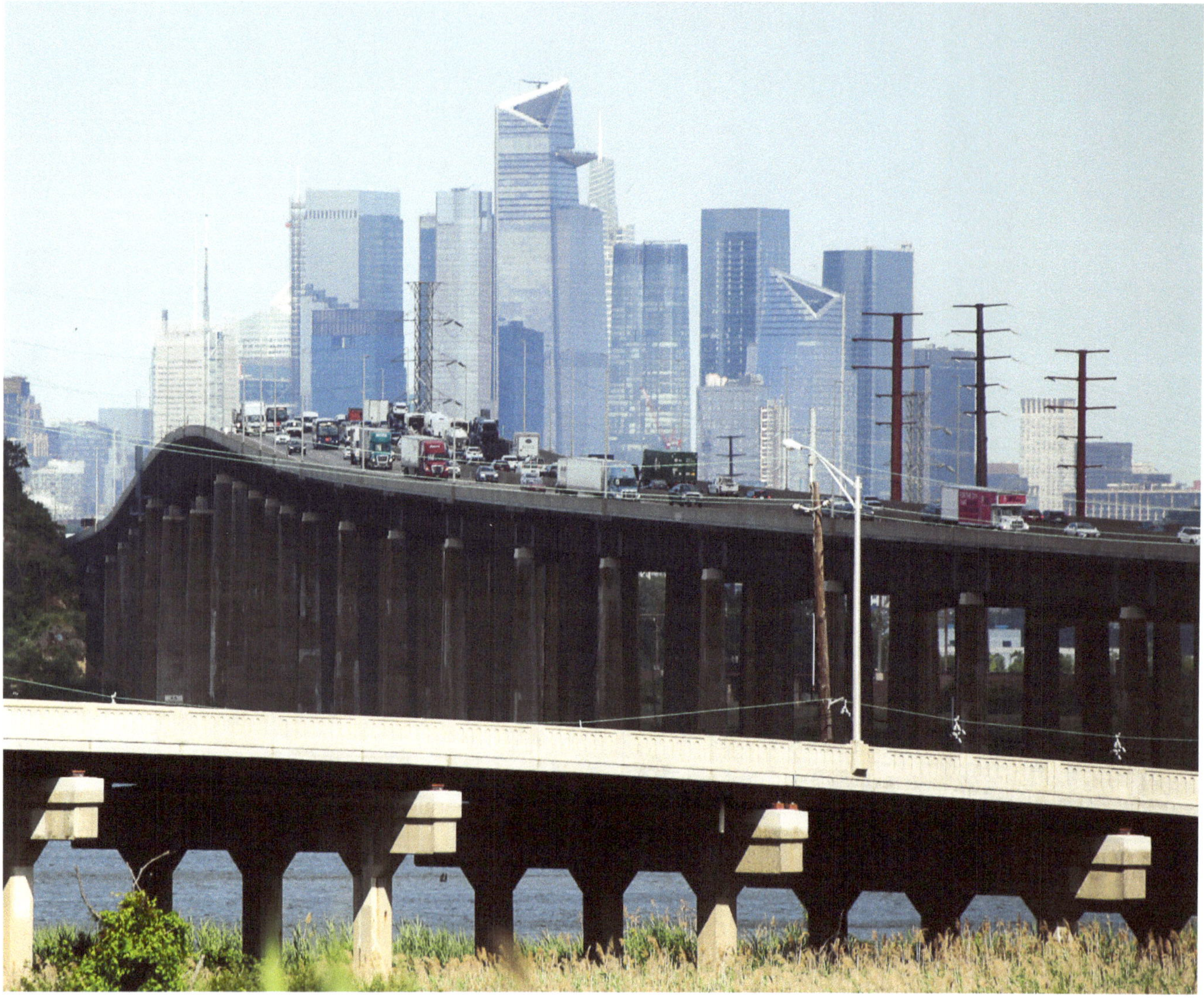

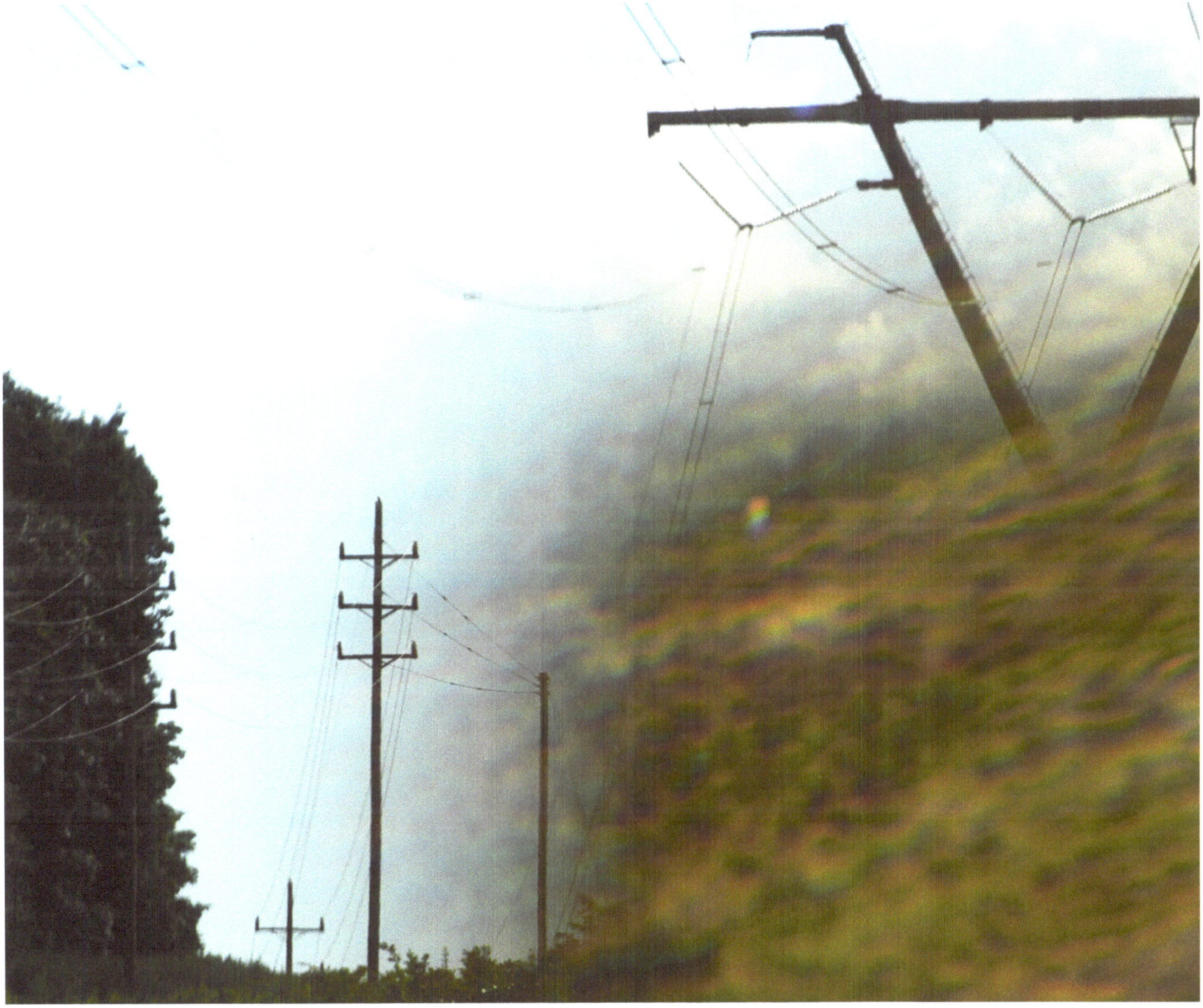

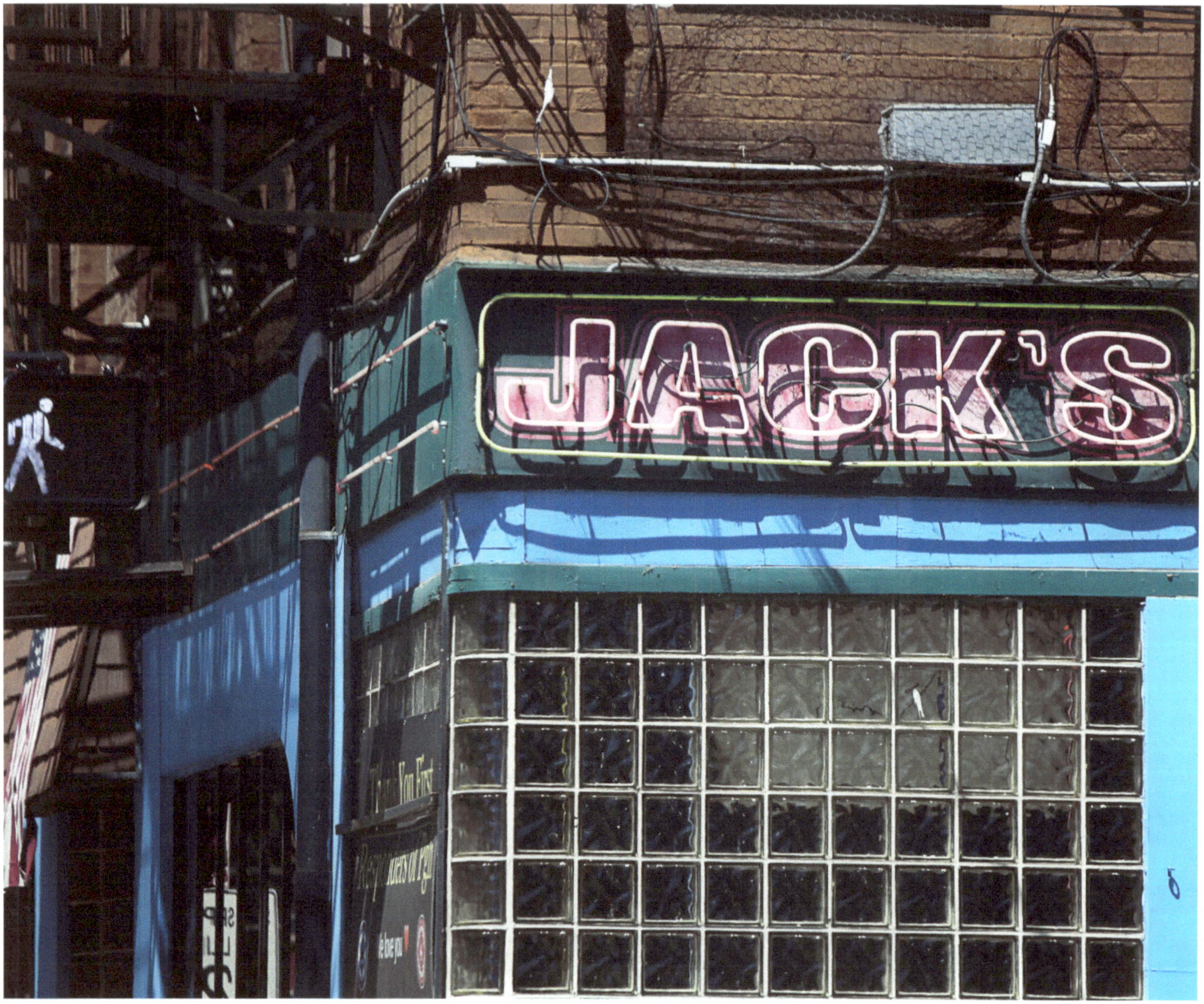
JACK'S

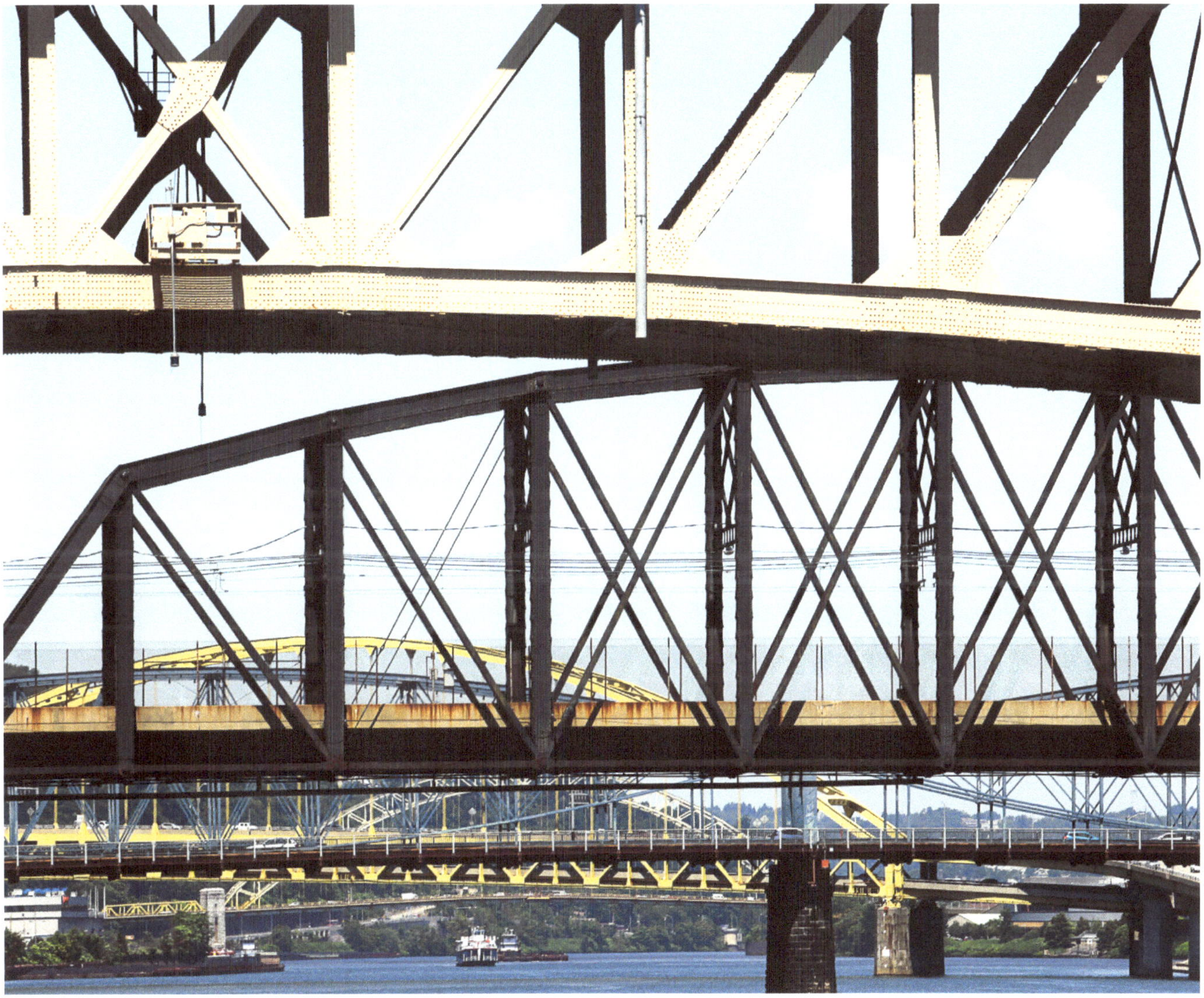

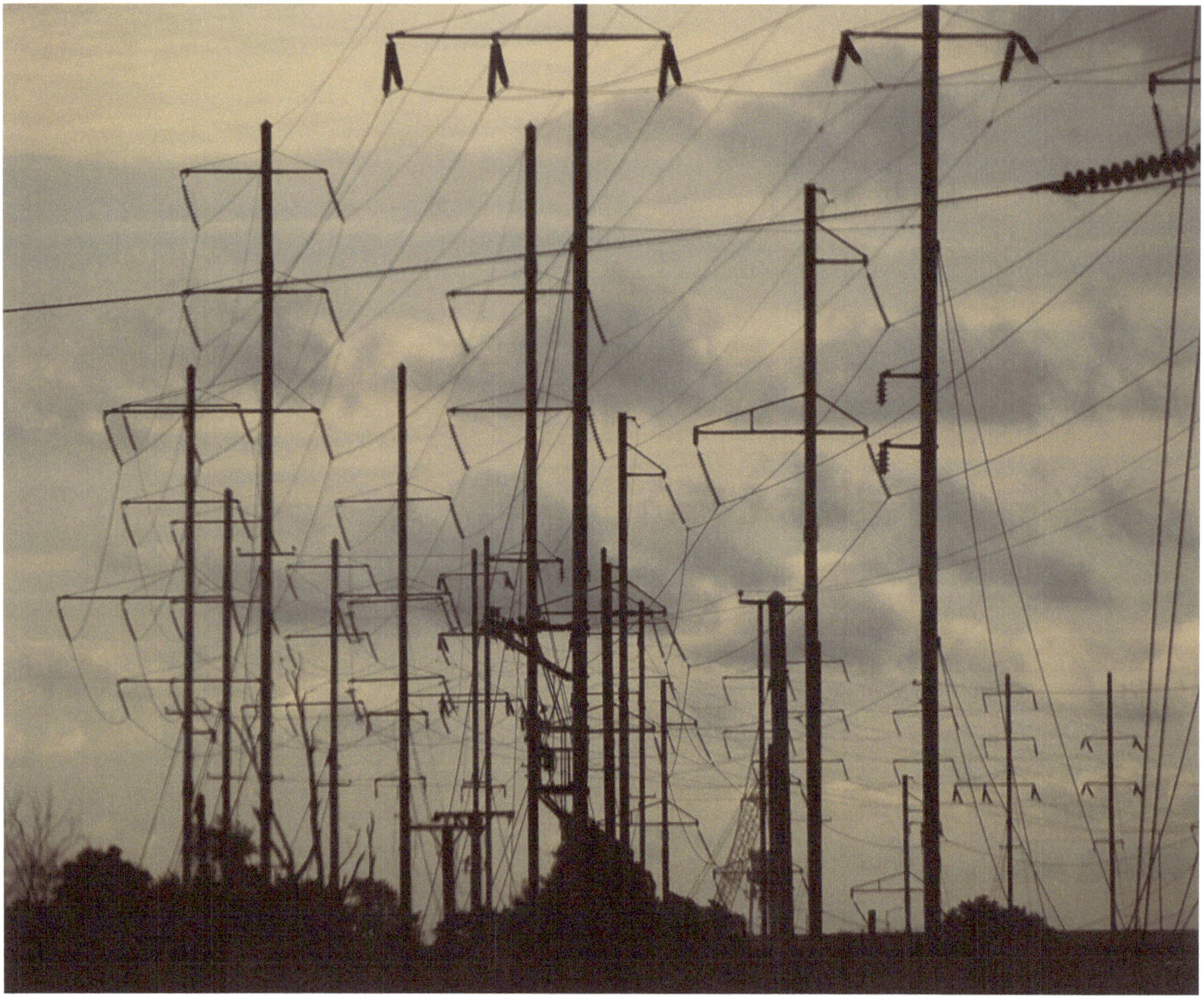

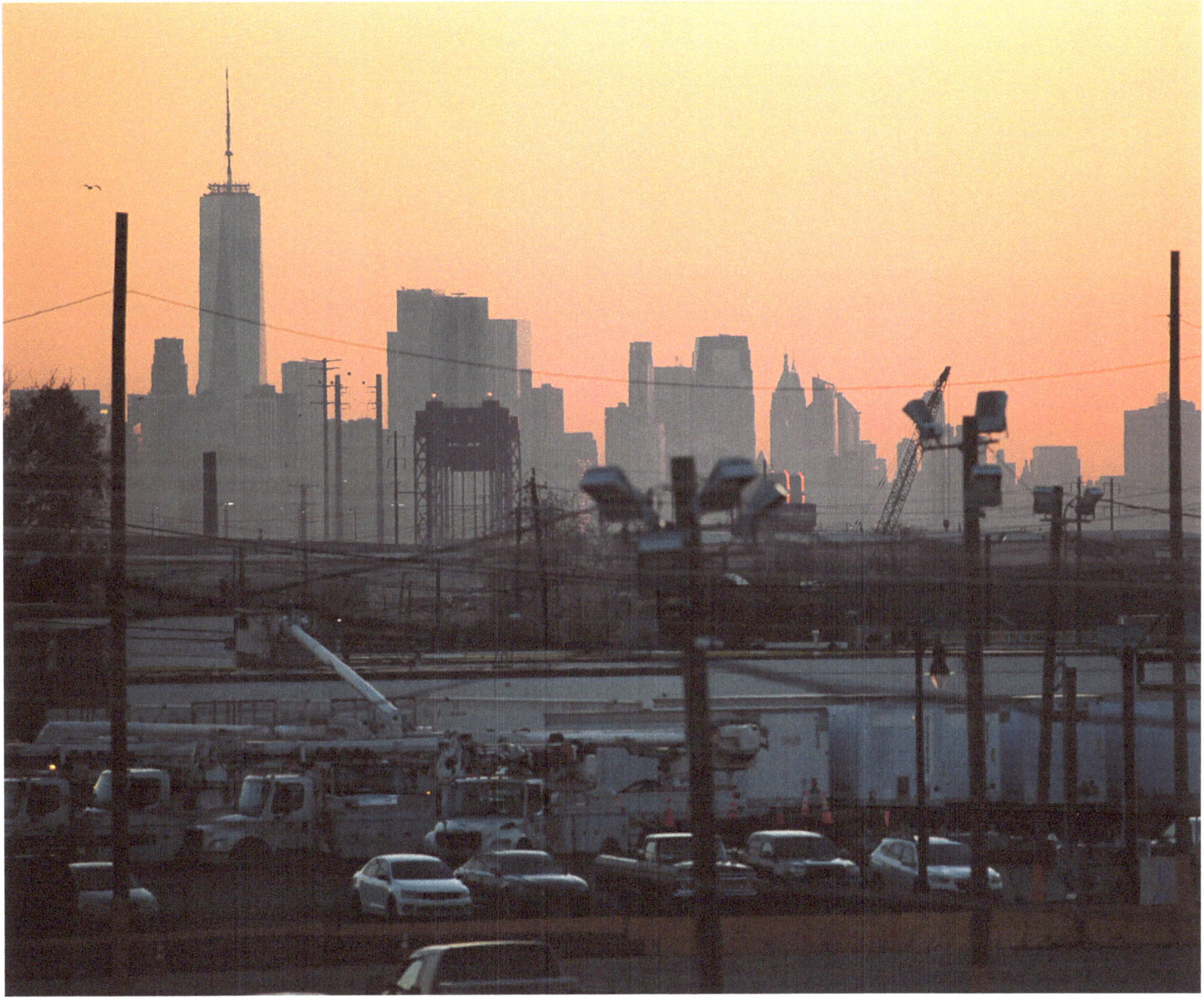

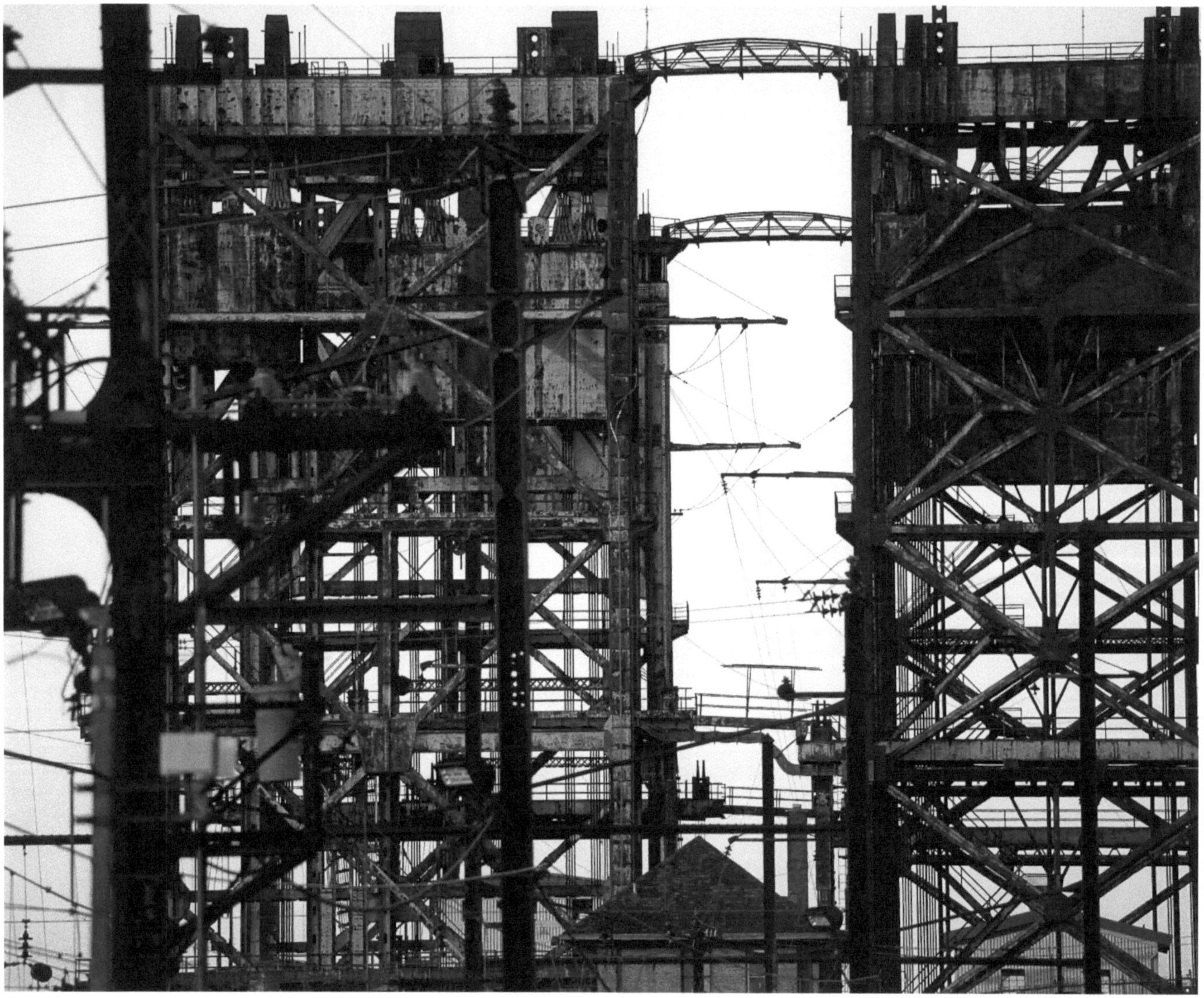

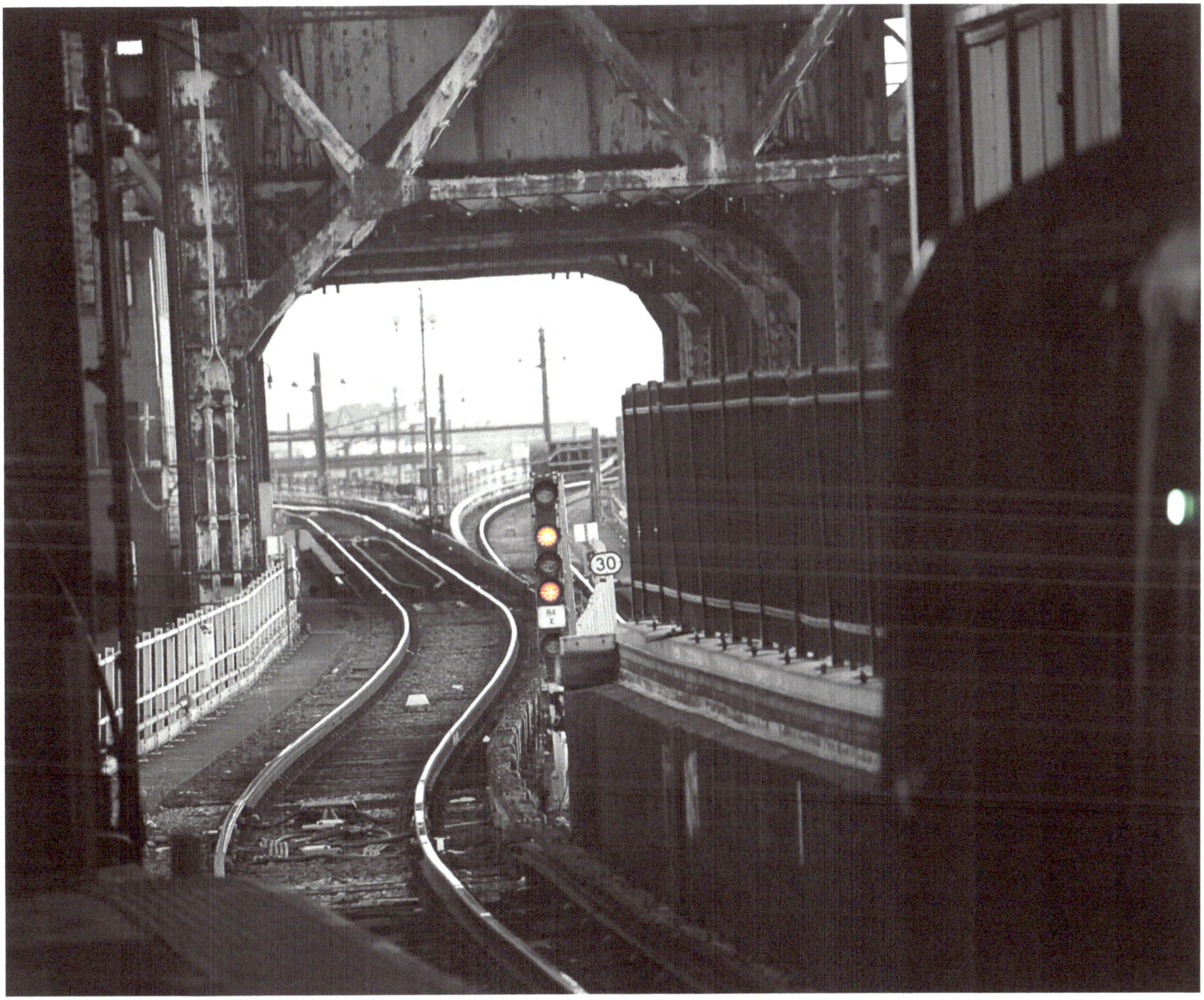
30

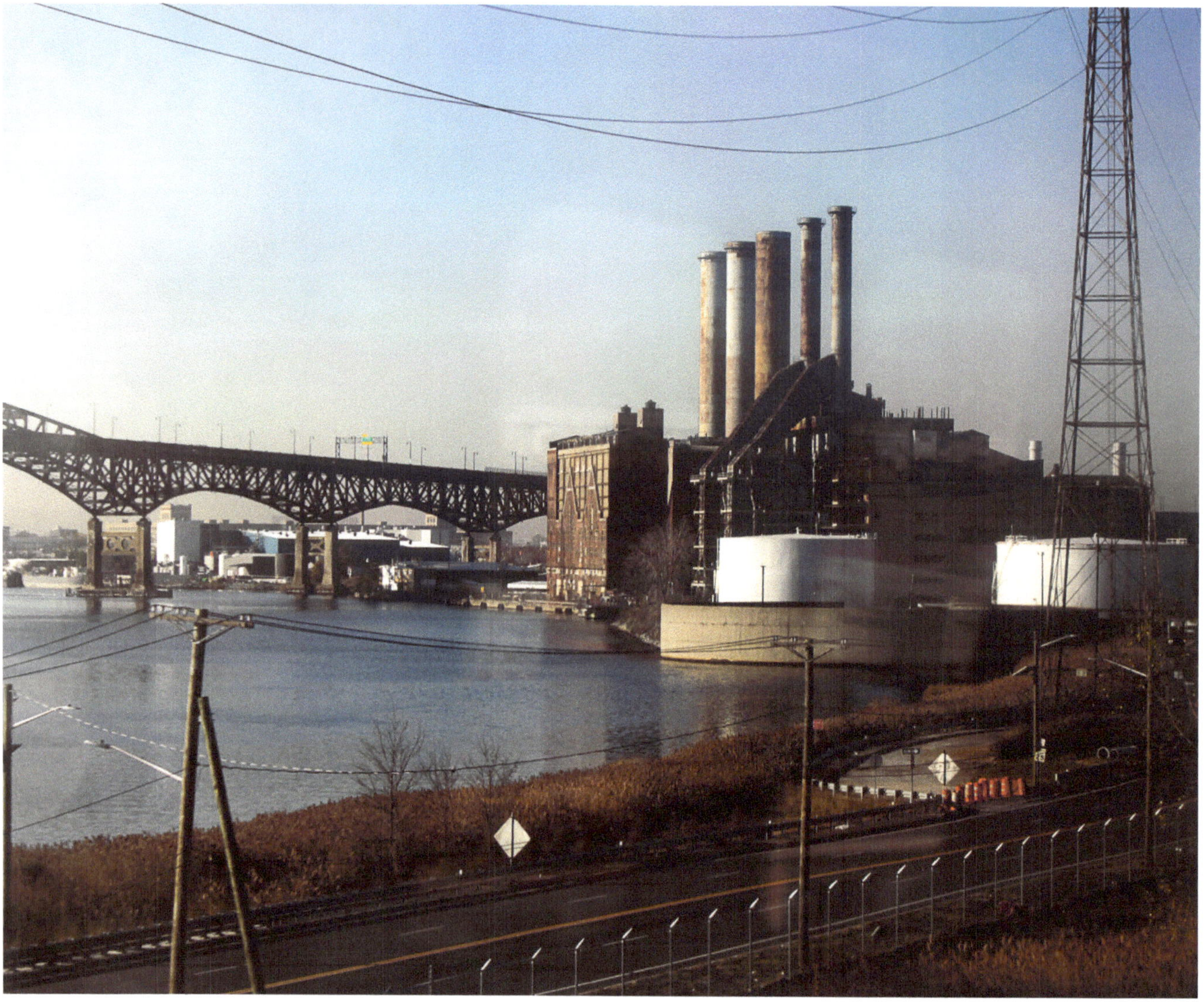

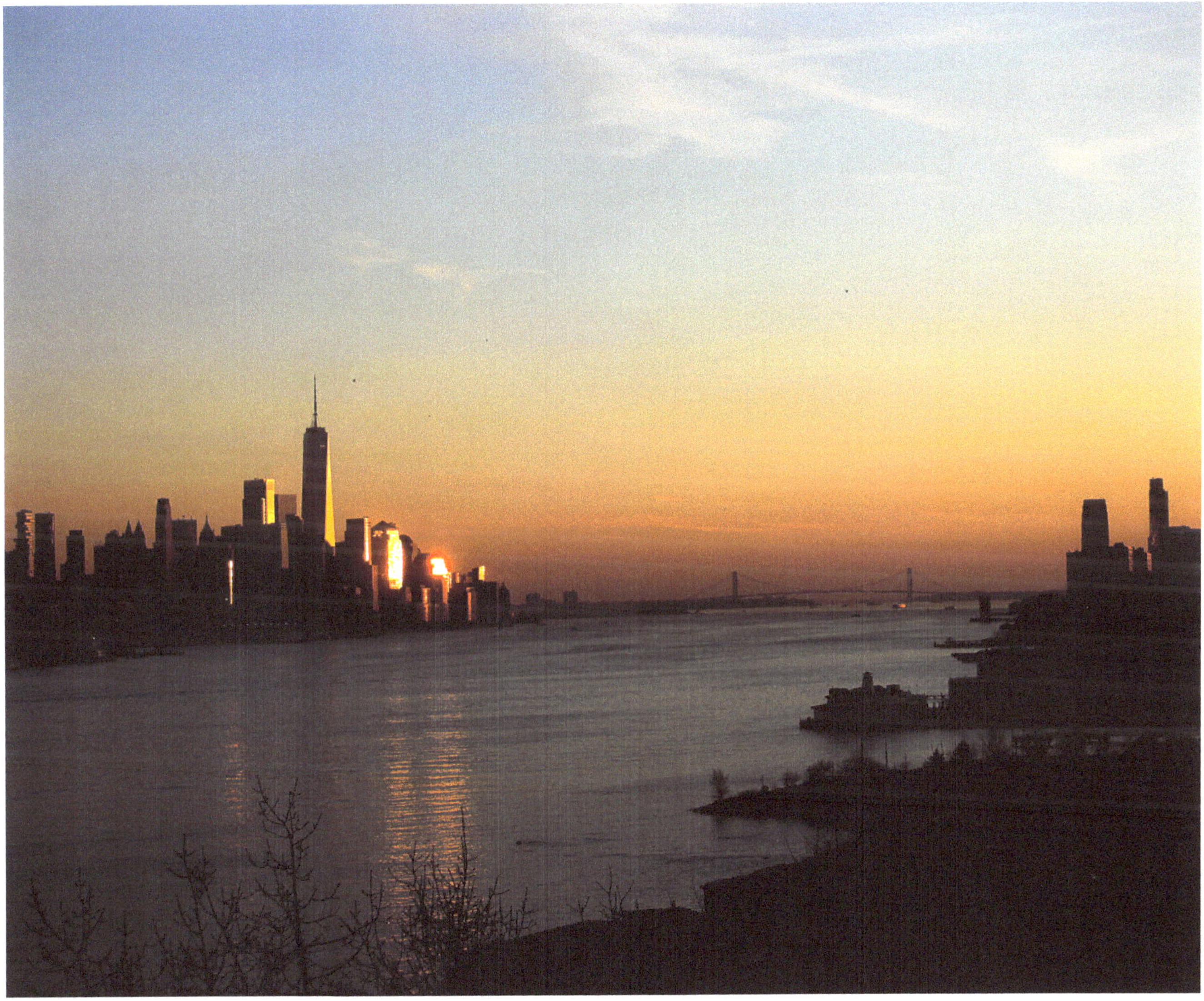

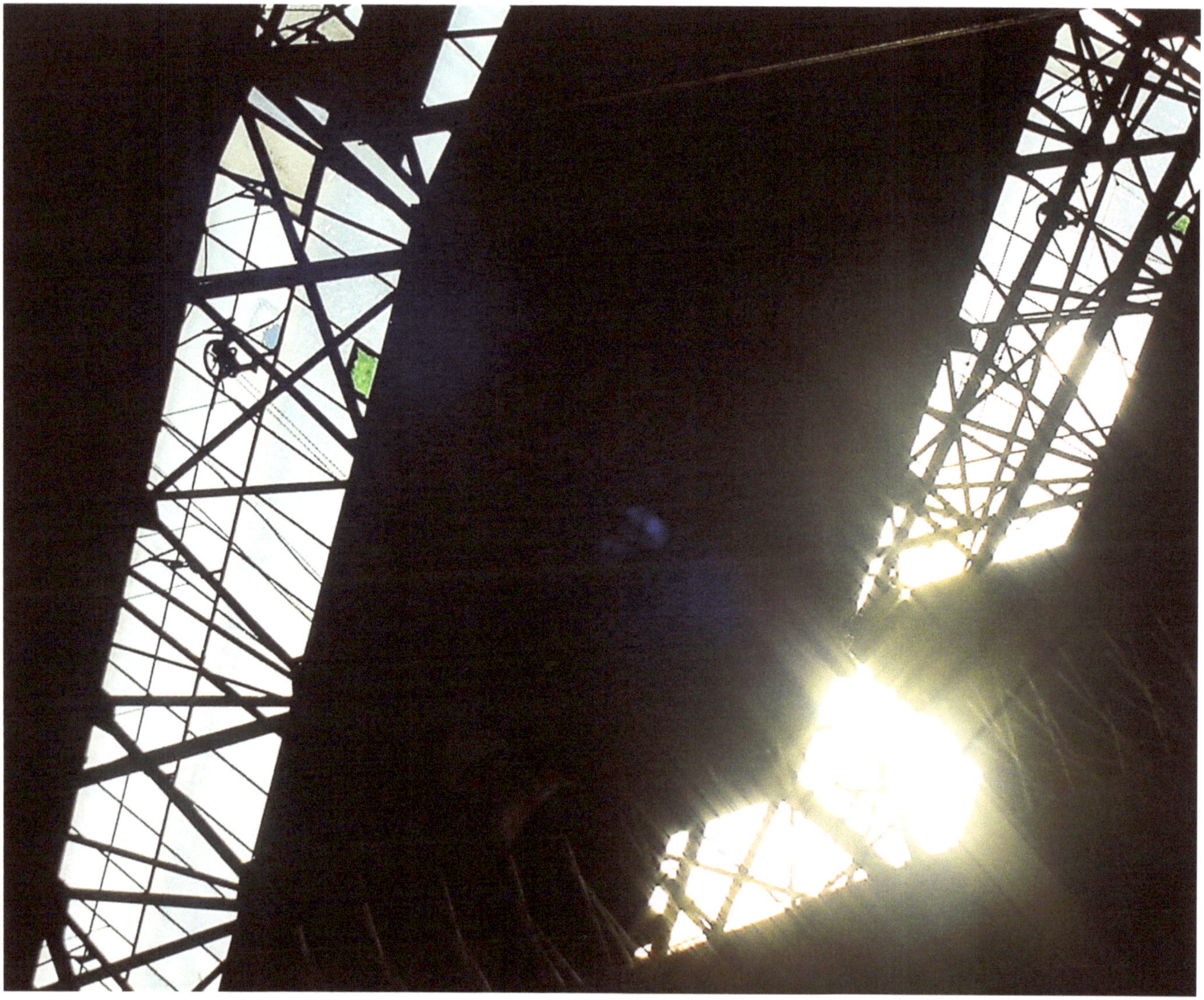

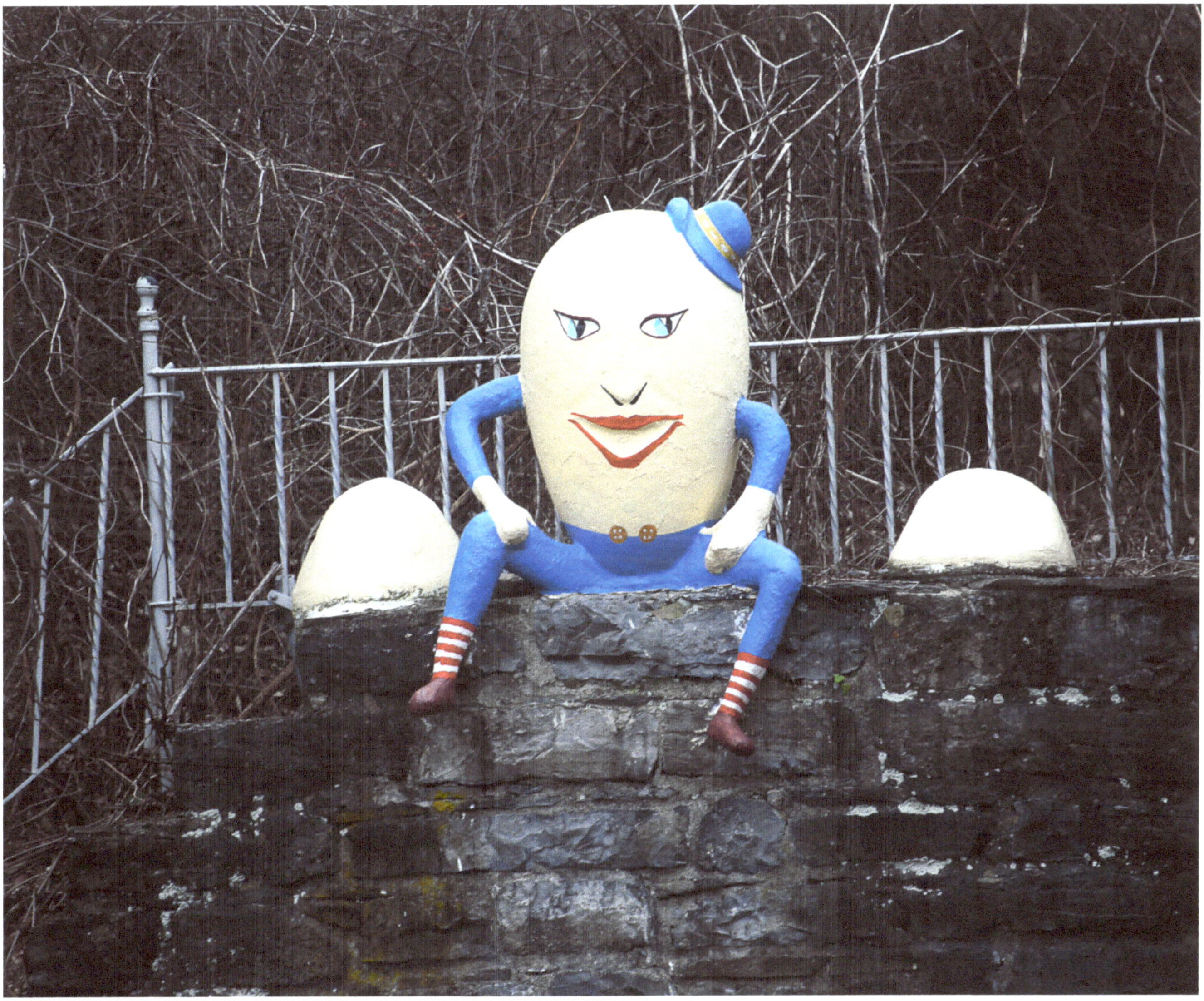

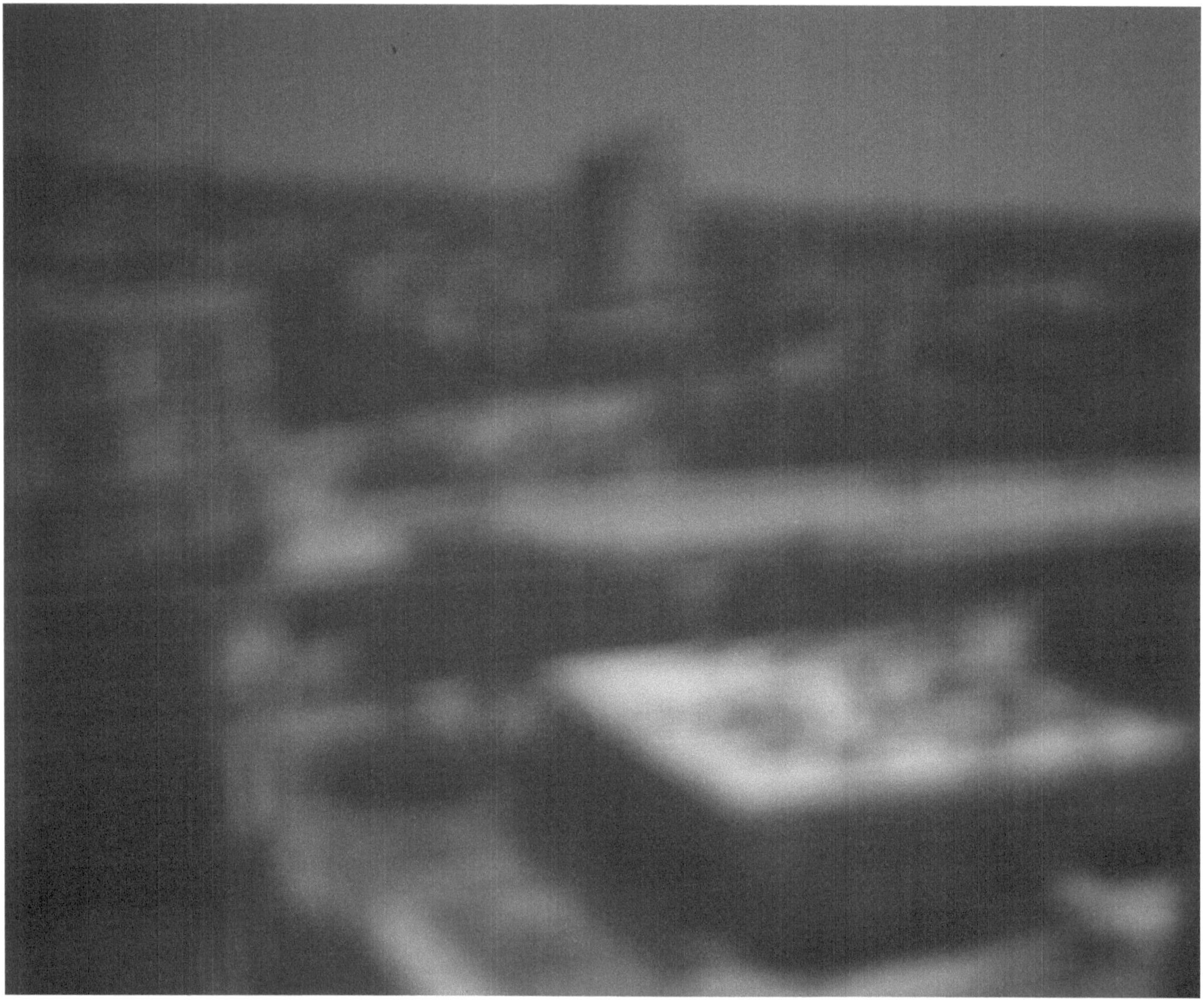

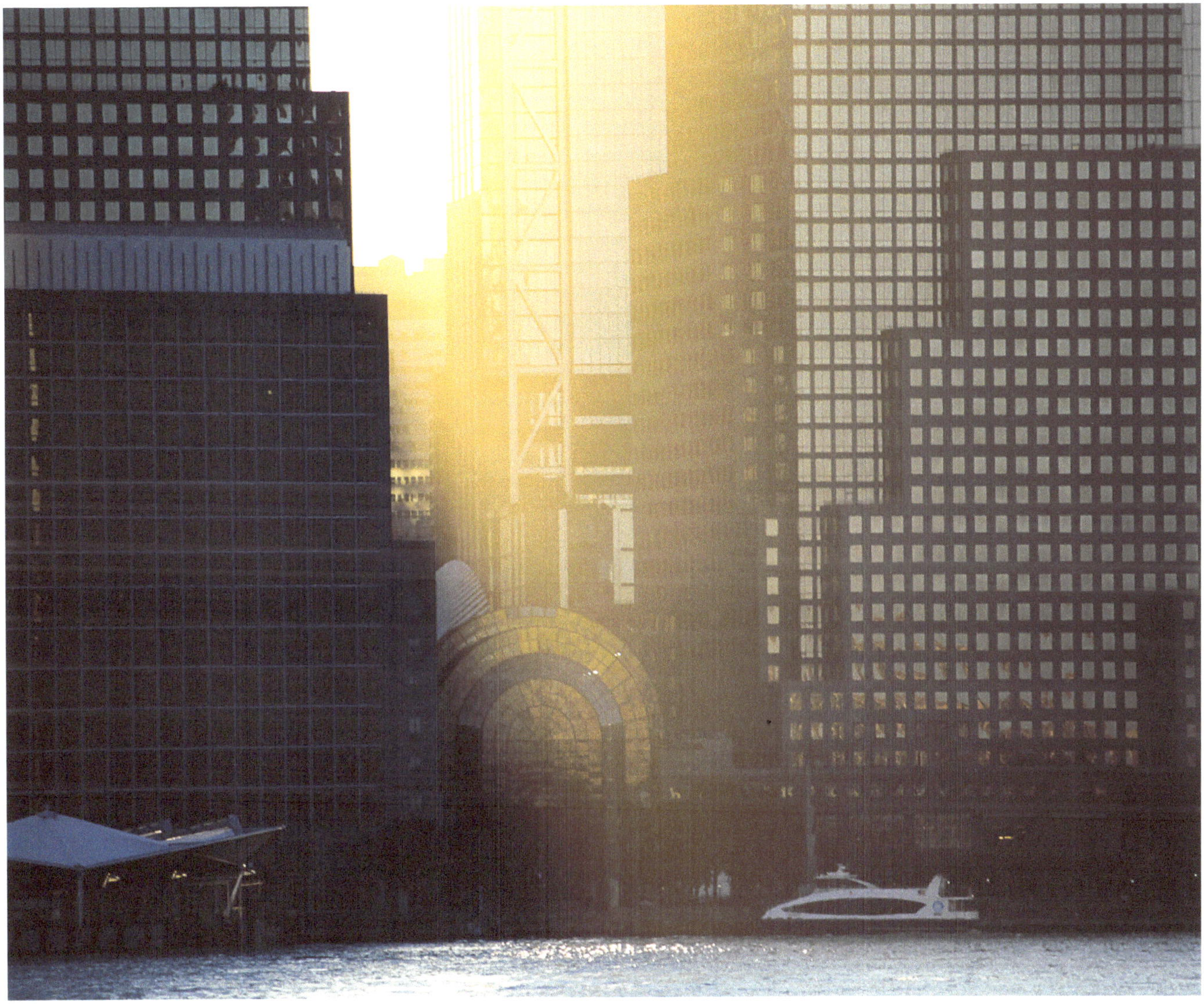

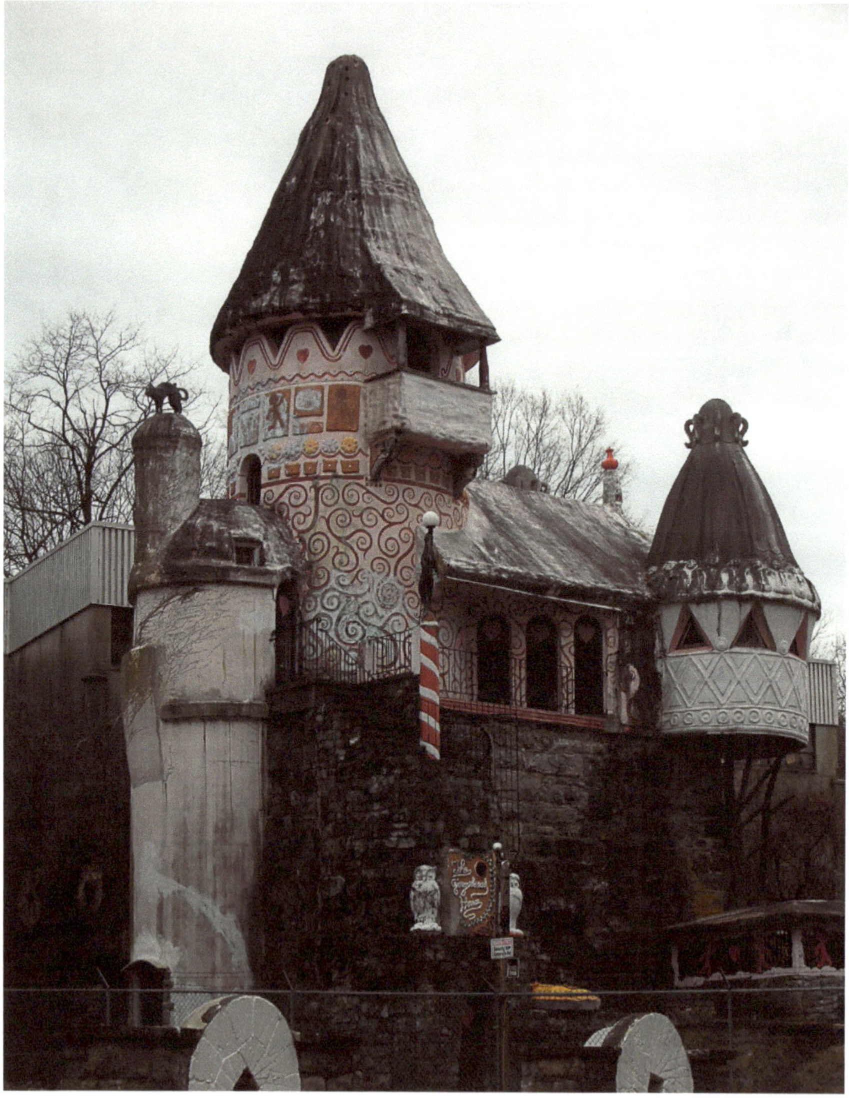

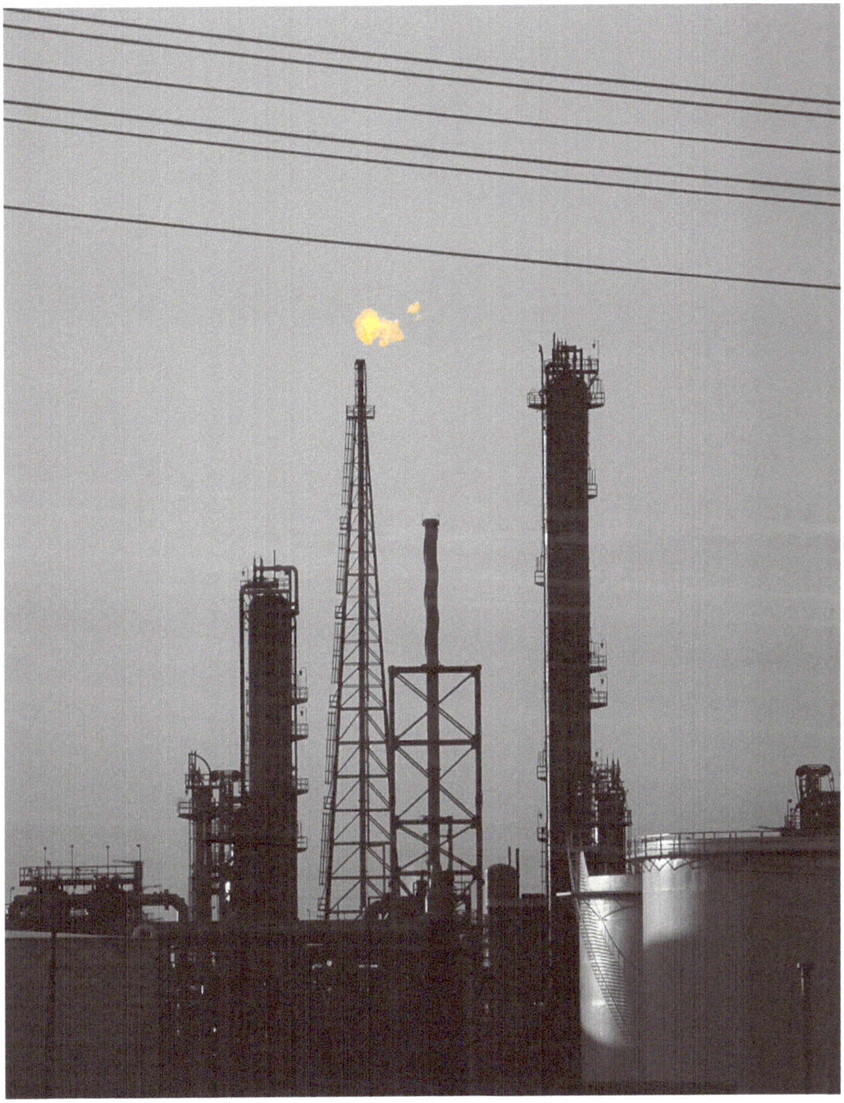

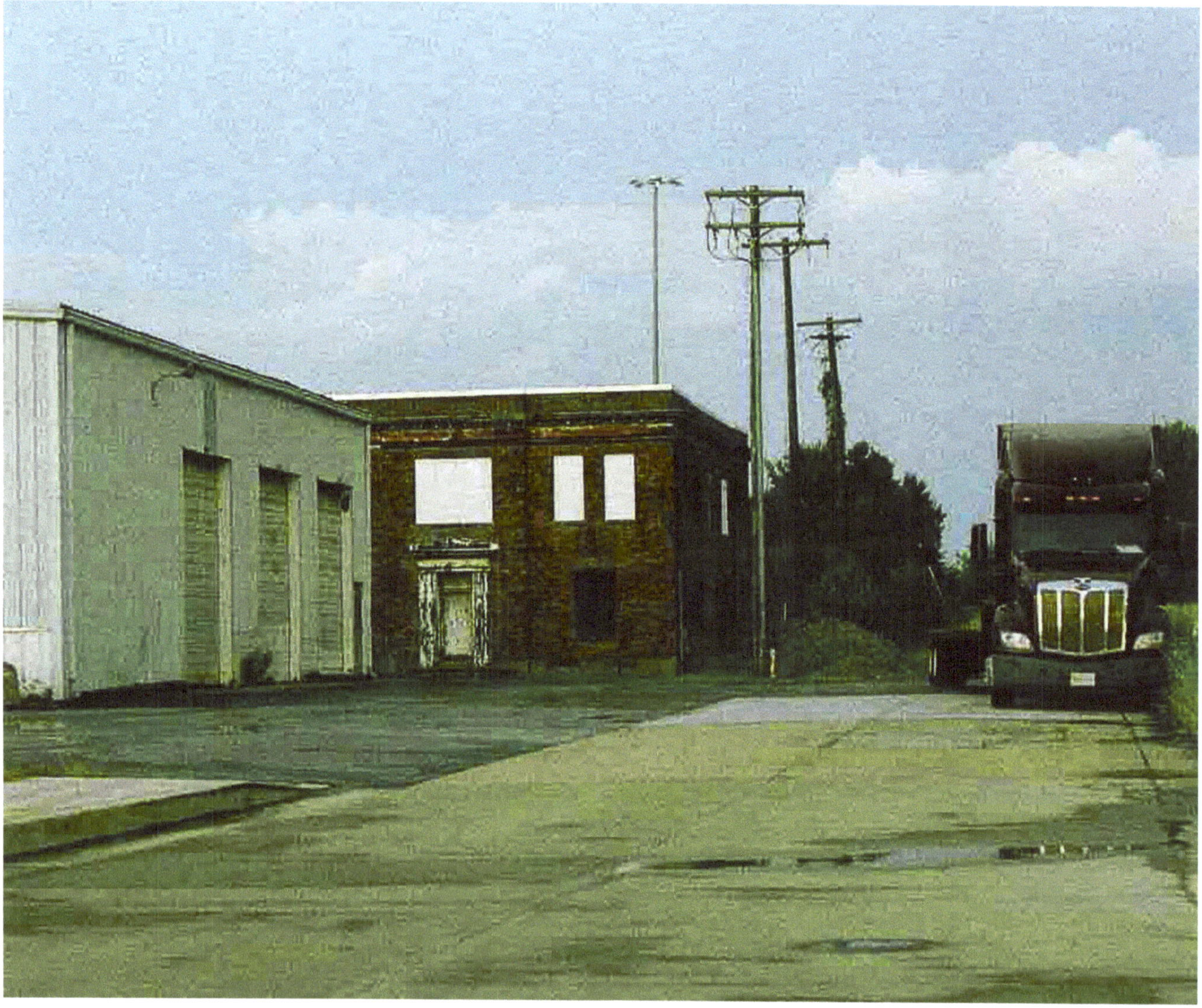

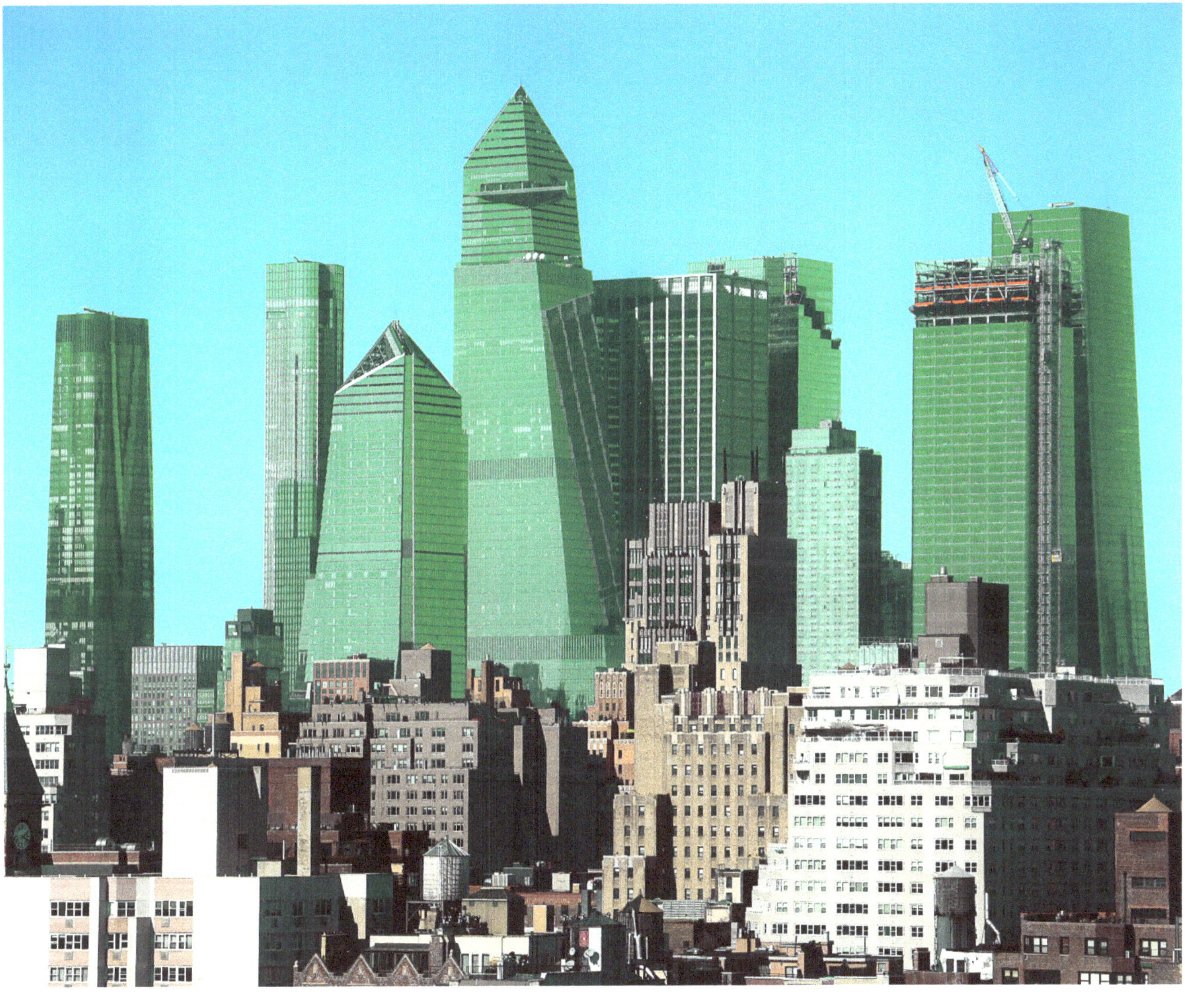

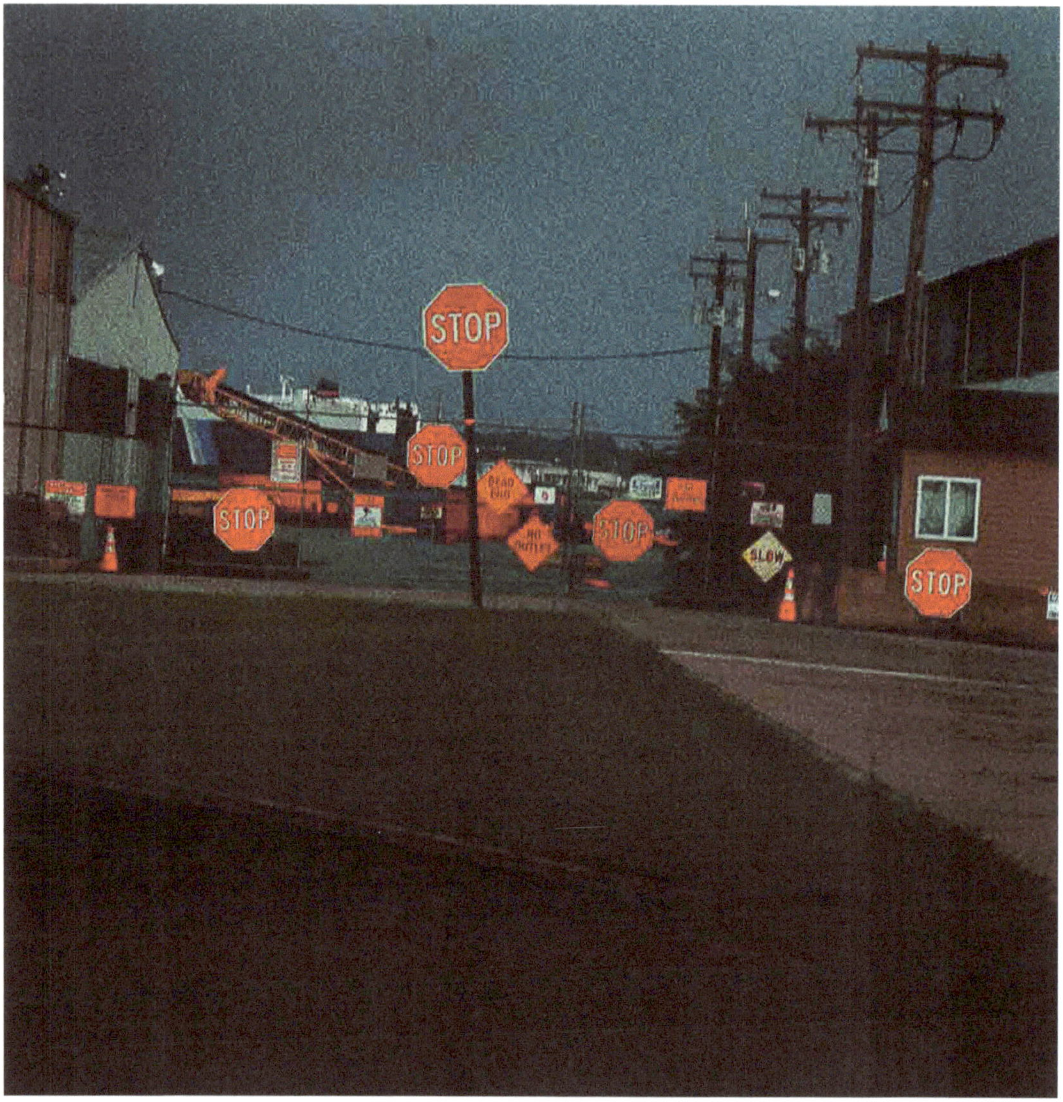
STOP
STOP
STOP
STOP
STOP
SLOW

www.ingramcontent.com/pod-product-compliance
Lightning Source LLC
Chambersburg PA
CBHW060834290526
45792CB00006BB/1925
9798884360594